DIVINE FEMININE ALIGNED

journal

*Activate Your Inner Goddess,
Live Your Purpose, and
Amplify Your Impact*

Compiled by
KENLYN KOLLEEN   ASTARA JANE ASHLEY

with contributions from 18 Divine Feminine Summit Speakers

FLOWER *of* LIFE PRESS

Divine Feminine Aligned Journal: Activate Your Inner Goddess, Live Your Purpose, and Amplify Your Impact

Copyright © 2022 Flower of Life Press

As of the time of initial publication, the URLs displayed in this book link or refer to existing websites on the Internet. Flower of Life Press, LLC is not responsible for, and should not be deemed to endorse or recommend, any website other than its own or any content available on the internet (including without limitation at any website, blog page, information page) that is not created by Flower of Life Press.

All rights reserved. No part of this publication may be reproduced, distributed, or transmitted in any form or by any means, including photocopying, recording, or other electronic or mechanical methods, without the prior written permission of the publisher, except in the case of brief quotations embodied in critical reviews and certain other noncommercial uses permitted by copyright law.

The content of this book is for general instruction only. Each person's physical, emotional, and spiritual condition is unique. The instruction in this book is not intended to replace or interrupt the reader's relationship with a physician or other mental health professional. Please consult your doctor for matters pertaining to your specific health.

Cover and Interior design by Molly Winjum, mollyandcocreative.com

Published by Flower of Life Press, *Hadlyme, CT.*
To contact the publisher, visit floweroflifepress.com

Library of Congress Control Number: Available upon request.

ISBN-13: 979-8-9864729-1-1

Printed in the United States of America

Goddess Rising

"This is for the women
Who have walked with hidden shame
Stirring like all is well
Though weighted down in pain

This is for her Inner Child
Who longs to forget
Her innocence stolen
Body, soul, and spirit rent
into pieces - fragments - broken - bent

This is for the Maiden
Longing to belong
To another
In hopes
to make right the darkened wrongs
Not realizing - blinded by oozing wounds
Her own innate delicious power
Thick within her womb

This is for the Mother
Breaking eons of fettered chains
For the children she has birthed
Through blood and breaths of change
She calls them Redemption
Regardless of their names

This is for the Crone
Who called her shattered pieces Home
To herself
To all her luminous bodies
Where she never dared to feel

Making strong her bones
Crushing ~ oppressors
With the swaying of her hips
Her hands soaring like doves
Honey dripping from her lips

This is for the Wild Woman
Who traversed the Underground
Leaving her footprints
While taming the Hellhounds
Like a seed breaking fallow ground
Emerging fruitful garden
No longer bound

By the nightmare of the past
Awakened from the Dream
Of Separation
SHE. IS. merging between realms.

This is for the woman, for the Goddess
For me
For you
Rising from our ashes
Making ALL things new~"

—MISHI MCCOY

Contents

INTRODUCTION
by Kenlyn Kolleen vii

GREEN TARA
by Astara Jane Ashley 1

SARASWATI
by Hemalayaa 15

MEDICINE WOMAN
by Rose Cole 29

SOPHIA
by Allison Conte 45

DANCING WITH DURGA
by Dana Damara 63

THE SACRED COURTESAN
by Dr. Saida Désilets 75

GAIA
by Clare DuBois 89

ATHENA
by Mayabello Fiennes 105

WARRIOR GODDESS
by Kimberly iMfezi Ingonyama Baskett .119

HIGH PRIESTESS EDGEWALKER
by Anahita Joon 135

THE QUEEN
by Kenlyn Kolleen 149

SARASWATI
by Jeanie Manchester 169

PHOENIX RISING
by Catherine Grace O'Connell 183

BLACK JAGUAR MEDICINE WOMAN
by Tanya Lynn 199

THE LOVER
by Ashley Fuller Rubin 215

DIVINE MOTHER NARAYANI
by Brahmankyrie Shanti 231

THE LOVE WARRIOR
by Lettie Sullivan 247

THE TEMPLE BODY PRIESTESS
by Sofiah Thom 259

LAKSHMI
by Patrina Wisdom 275

Introduction

By Kenlyn Kolleen

Welcome, Sister, to the *Divine Feminine Aligned Journal.*

Just like the Divine Feminine Summit, this journal is a collaboration borne out of the sisterhood. When Astara Jane Ashley asked me if her publishing company Flower of Life Press could partner with me and the Divine Feminine Summit to create a book, I enthusiastically said *Yes!* and envisioned a ritual handbook, which is now in your hands. I know you're going to love what we've put together for you.

At the end of 2019 I was inspired to take my women's empowerment work to the next level and curate my first Divine Feminine Summit. My vision was, and still is, to support women to align with their true purpose so they can increase their impact and income. It dawned on me that the Divine Feminine archetypes, goddesses, and avatars already provide us with the support we need to actualize that vision. Collectively I call them archetypes. They are badass, fierce, divine, grounded, accepting, open, loving, compassionate, and trusting.

Archetypes are energies that live in our collective unconscious. Through eons of time since early humans worshiped the mother as the source of Life, the codes of the Divine Feminine have been hidden inside every person, man or woman, revealing themselves in culture after culture to those who have eyes to see or ears to hear.

Mythological literature makes it clear that these archetypes must be evoked, otherwise they remain dormant. The Divine Feminine Summit serves as an invocation, a quickening, an activation of these archetypal energies. Some archetypes, the speaker and I invented. Others were drawn from the pantheon of the Divine Feminine in cultures and epochs where she reigned supreme, such as India and Egypt. You may recognize some of them in this journal as you revisit the activations from each of the speakers, and some may be entirely new to you.

In mid-January of 2020, I launched the first summit. While I knew this would be so powerful, I had no way of knowing how important these activations would be to a world that was a couple months away from a major tectonic shift that would change us forever. The summit was a huge hit, and women all over the world experienced major life transformations as they activated these potent energies inside their own being. I took a poll to find out which archetype was most impactful. Although all of them had so many votes, the one that struck the loudest chord turned out to be prescient—the goddess of death and rebirth herself, Kali Ma.

Looking back on this data, I saw something about our sisterhood that I didn't understand fully until that moment: WE ARE HER. We are the eyes, ears, hands, nose, breasts, feet, arms of the manifestation of the Divine Feminine on Earth. As such, of course, we knew what was to come. Of course, the

– Introduction –

Indian goddess of death and rebirth, who cuts heads off and drinks the blood of her enemies (unconsciousness) moved us most. We knew.

As I approached the 2021 summit, I was on the edge of my seat wondering what Divine Feminine theme would emerge. My first scheduled interview revealed the answer: sexual power. I thought, "Holy wow, the Divine Feminine is reclaiming her power through our wombs, yonis, and feminine bodies." I was shaking with so much joy and activation, I knew it was true. Women reclaimed—and are still reclaiming—so much of what was lost through patriarchal shaming and repression. The power of *her* is being unleashed in our bodies. Again, we're being prepared for what's to come.

This is the context in which you find the *Divine Feminine Aligned Journal.*

These activations work in layers. They're not "one and done" but are more like a hurricane spiral, constantly revealing themselves. The more you work with them, the more they will reveal themselves. Let this journal be your sacred muse to go deeper with these archetypes.

The Divine Feminine has just begun to RISE—she's just getting started. Our job is to shed as much conditioning as we can so that we can hear her voice and act accordingly. The world as we knew it pre-2020 will never return. The question for us now is, "What will we create?" I believe in my bones that the Divine Feminine is the secret hope of humanity. She is a frequency, not a destination or a place. As frequency creates matter, so shall the Divine Feminine frequency create the New Earth.

Enjoy these activations with your whole body, heart, and mind as you activate your inner goddess, live your purpose, and amplify your impact.

May it be so.

In Divine Love,

Kenlyn Kolleen
Encinitas, CA

Green Tara

by Astara Jane Ashley

> "Tara is without a doubt the most beloved female deity in Tibetan Buddhism, revered for her swiftness in helping those who rely on her. She has been described as a Buddha for our modern age, a sublime personification of compassion and wisdom in female form at a time when sorrow and suffering seem to be increasing everywhere. Of all the Buddhas, Tara is the most accessible."
>
> —H.E. Venerable Zasep Tulku Rinpoche,
> *Tara in the Palm of Your Hand*

My life's path has included many shifts and pivots along the way, and Green Tara has taught me how to release internal narratives and external drama so I can instead choose peace and presence. She has shown me that when we are willing and ready to consciously shift from fear to love, we will clearly see the gifts that were hiding in plain sight.

When Covid started, I decided to enroll in an online "Green Tara" painting course created by an amazing woman—Whitney Freya. Whitney is a transformational coach and incredible artist. Having worked with Whitney to publish her books, I was confident that something would emerge from the course experience that would transform me.

Whitney's course was my introduction to the energies of the goddess Green Tara and her 21 faces (or aspects). It was exactly what I needed to break through some blocks and expose the old, sludgy layers of unworthiness and mother-wounding that were holding me back.

I was familiar with the energies of the Goddess of Compassion—Kuan Yin—and I soon realized that Green Tara was another variation of her. I was open to receiving the medicine from Green Tara and the blessings that she showed me then—and continues to show me—around mothering, compassion, surrender, forgiveness, self-acceptance, and fierce love. When I call upon Tara, she enters into my field and the inner sanctuary of my heart. I feel her working through me.

Green Tara is known as our true Mother—the female Buddha Mother Tara: She who gives birth to and develops our enlightened mind and reveals herself in different forms and qualities of the enlightened mind, helping us to overcome all fears and difficulties on the way.

Her color green represents the universal frequency of healing, regeneration, and growth. She embodies the healing energy of release from fear and ignorance. The healing energy of Green Tara's 21 different aspects brings awareness and relief from negativity and replaces it with swift blessings, abundance, and spiritual boons.

HERE ARE THE 21 DIFFERENT FACES OF TARA:

Tara 1 - Heroic Red Tara

Tara 2 - Moonlight White Tara

Tara 3 - Golden Colour Tara

Tara 4 - Golden Tara of Crown Victorious

Tara 5 - Tara Proclaiming the Sound of HUM

Tara 6 - Tara Victorious over the Three Levels of the World

Tara 7 - Tara Who Crushes Adversaries

Tara 8 - Tara Who Gives Supreme Spiritual Power

Tara 9 - Tara of the Khadira Fragrant Forest (Principle Green Tara)

Tara 10 - Tara Who Dispels All Suffering

Tara 11 - Tara Who Summons All Beings and Dispels Misfortune

Tara 12 - Tara Who Grants Prosperity and Brings about Auspicious Circumstances

Tara 13 - Tara the Complete Ripener

Tara 14 - Wrathful, Shaking and Frowning Tara

Tara 15 - Tara the Great Peaceful One Who Provides Virtues and Goodness

Tara 16 - Tara Destroyer of All Attachment

Tara 17 - Tara Accomplisher of Joy and Bliss

Tara 18 - Victorious Tara Who Increases Realizations

Tara 19 - Tara, Extinguisher of All Suffering

Tara 20 - Tara, Source of All-Powerful Attainments

Tara 21 - Tara of the Perfection of Wisdom and Compassion

I began by moving through each face of Tara over the course of 21 days. Each day I painted on top of the layer from the previous day with the new color associated with that day's face. Through this process, I cultivated my skills of diving in, trusting, and then letting go. I would add to what was already there, yet ultimately, a whole new layer would emerge. This practice of detaching from the outcome and trusting the process also allowed me to face my inner critic and shadows of comparison with other artists in the class who were "better" than me. I processed and released all triggers and memories as they emerged. Tara was helping me alchemize!

Green Tara was showing herself to me in many new ways and I began chanting her mantra, Om Tara Tu Tare, Ture Soha, which means "I prostrate to Tara the liberator, mother of all the victorious ones." Chanting her mantra is very relaxing and comforting!

I chanted to Green Tara any chance I could, whether I was in the shower, working, or driving. It was an endless prayer! In fact, one morning, I was awoken by the sound of my own voice chanting in my sleep! The most awe-inspiring moment was when I realized that I ALREADY had statues of Green Tara in my home in three different places, but hadn't even realized who she was!

The painting process and chanting were visceral and allowed me to experience Green Tara in my body, without my mind running the show. Now, when I enlist her support as part of my spiritual team, she provides peace, passion, and a remembrance of my true, empowered self. I keep her close to me by having fresh, live flowers and plants in my home. When I sit outside and soak up her gorgeous green frequency in nature, Green Tara helps me hold space for myself, for my family, for our planet and for humanity with open-hearted compassion. She helps me to embody the frequency of divine mother and unconditional love.

I am not surprised that Spirit decided to show up for me through painting Green Tara because making art had always been the portal into my soul where I could experience presence, release myself from the shackles of the matrix, and hang out in the creative zone of kairos, or timelessness… I never wanted to leave that space.

Today, with years of healing work behind me, I know my mythic purpose: To walk the path of the open heart, shine my light, and radiate love so that I can serve other people and our planet from that place. I am here to hold a massive space for lightworkers to share their message with the world through their books, art, and self-expressed truth.

We all know that stories of women have been suppressed for EONS. But do you realize that WE are the ones we have been waiting for?

My miracle—my vision—is to share 1 million women's stories with the world. We are here to tell the stories. To carry the wisdom forward, creating space for the next generation to use it and build upon it—for the good of ALL LIFE.

Writing is a pathway into the soul where the alchemy of healing happens. The process itself is so transformational; I witness many of my authors write their story and the shift in them from day one to their launch date is profound! These women have elevated, found their confidence and owned their power. They are holding and emanating more light and sacred space. They are ready to walk into the room holding their book and themselves in the highest regard, owning their unique gifts yet detached from the outcome—no longer apologizing for existing. Their inner Tara is fully activated and shining, heart open and sovereign.

– Divine Feminine Aligned Journal –

I have claimed my inner queen and my throne with the help of Tara. Her energies have helped me to create congruity between my inner and the external worlds, and have brought abundance in all areas of my life. Green Tara has helped me shine my light and raise my vibration so that now I see something new being reflected back at me—the manifestation of my desires! Her presence has activated me to heal my relationship with my daughters and my mother. She teaches me about compassion and how to hold it for myself and for others. As soon as I melt into compassion, my heart opens and I am in that vibration of love—and not distracted. Compassion is the thing that pulls me back to my center point; the place inside that is stable, grounded, and awake.

Have you found your voice and discerned your message? When you choose to write your story, you will empower yourself to speak up, add to a new cultural narrative, create an archive of your wisdom, and truly LIVE your legacy.

You will claim your throne as the Queen of your Queendom in your sovereign truth as a clear and luminous channel for the energies of the Divine Feminine to flow through you. And as you continue to alchemize your shadows, rewire, and remember the ways of LOVE via your writing, know that you are ushering in for the collective a new frequency of love that our world desperately needs to embrace.

So, sister, I ask you now, who is on your walls? What art is in your space? What are the color frequencies you've brought into your space? What are the energies you feel that are new inside of you?

I didn't realize until I was complete with those 21 days of painting Green Tara that my own name, "Astara" contains the name "Tara" in it.

Of course, it does!

Green Tara has been with me all along.

Activation

Begin by simply bringing Tara's energy into your space. Go outside and find some flowers or greenery to decorate the inside of your home. Bring in the life of nature. Place some of the green and natural items on your altar. Wear the color green to acknowledge that the love and power of Green Tara lives in you.

*Next, listen to my favorite version of Green Tara's chant, or pick one of your own. Play the song over and over, at least three times or for at least 15 minutes. Have fun—there is no perfect way to chant, only YOUR way. Release all perfectionism and allow the sound vibration to attune you to Tara's energy. My favorite playlist of Green Tara music is on Spotify here: **https://spoti.fi/3ENx2wc***

– *Divine Feminine Aligned Journal* –

Journal and Integrate

Write the mantra "Om Tara Tu Tare Ture Soha" 108 times.

After singing the mantra and writing it 108 times, how do you feel energetically? Do you feel your spirit lifted?

– Divine Feminine Aligned Journal –

Free Gift

YOUR WRITING ROADMAP: 3 PHASES TO WRITING A BESTSELLER THAT LEAVES YOUR AUDIENCE RAVING!

To receive this training in your inbox, simply fill out this short, 2-question application to our writing course, "Divine Writing Journey" (no obligation to join).

Apply here >> divinewritingjourney.com

GET PUBLISHED IN AN ANTHOLOGY!

Here's your opportunity to share YOUR story!

Details here >> turningpointstory.com

Biography

ASTARA JANE ASHLEY

> *"I hold my authors in the center-point between deep support and accountability, meeting the needs of the moment so that they can ignite the flame that creates resonance in their writing and breaks through any blocks or resistance. It is there that they discover a whole new level of aliveness, abundance, commitment to their path, and connection to themselves and their readers."*
>
> ~Astara

With years of deep healing and embodiment work behind her, Astara knows herself and her sacred purpose: to midwife women's stories and wisdom—through their books—into a new cultural narrative that includes the voice of the Divine Feminine.

Her background in corporate publishing, Transpersonal psychotherapy, and Art therapy offers Astara's clients the support they need to unearth their soul's message, open their creative channel, and write their book from a place of authenticity and trust in the divine plan of their own becoming.

Astara's teachings are based on ancient knowledge and feminine principles such as unity, connection, love, inclusivity, collaboration, community, equitability, and expansion. She has immersed herself in esoteric wisdom traditions as a Priestess Initiate of the 13 Moon Mystery School and as a

Scent/Anointing Priestess. Astara has studied with a 5th generation Essential Oils alchemist in Cairo, Egypt, and worked with sacred plant medicines and Shamans for over a decade.

Astara knows the hurdles in navigating relationships, self-care, time with family, and running a 6-figure business. Her motto is: "Every creation must result in a win-win for all involved." Her online writer's group, Published Priestess, is a global sisterhood of authors who, in a safe space and strongly-held container, share their truth, write from the heart, and transform themselves by transmuting energy and embodying their higher self.

Astara is the creator of the best-selling "New Feminine Evolutionary" collaborative book series, consisting of 7 books and hundreds of contributing authors. Through these potent writing collaborations, she helps women claim their power, voice, and visibility as leaders in their field.

Flower of Life Press is devoted to dismantling systems of oppression and centering the voices of women of color. Our bestselling anthology, "Ancient-Future Unity: Reclaim your Roots, Liberate your Lineage, Live a Legacy of Love," is now available and features the raw and real stories of 26 black feminine leaders.

Astara recently birthed a new publishing imprint for bestselling author of the Magdalene Trilogy, Kathleen McGowan, called Asherah Press. Together, Astara and Kathleen have linked arms through their common mission to support the rise of the Divine Feminine through single-author books, anthologies, courses, events, and sacred travel.

FLOWER *of* LIFE PRESS

The Flower of Life Press logo contains an ancient symbol representing the energy of creation and the flow of potential. It is a reminder of the interconnectedness of life and the beauty of the universe. With this engine of transformation as its symbolic essence, Flower of Life Press is dedicated and devoted to the emerging voices of leaders and changemakers—all of those beings who seek a home for the conversation of change.

Learn more at **floweroflifepress.com**.

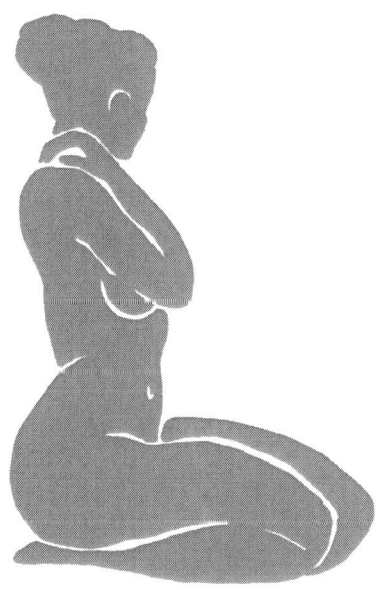

Saraswati

THE GODDESS OF COMMUNICATION, HIGHER LEARNING, AND CREATIVITY

by Hemalayaa

Saraswati and Brahma, her consort, are the deities of creation—the first step in birthing anything. I believe that we're all artists; we're all creative beings, but we might have shut that down at some point. For a long time, my creativity was blocked. I thought that only painters or musicians were artists. What I learned was that we are all artists! When Saraswati came into my life, she showed me how to call my creativity into manifestation and take it into service.

The question is, which deity are we working for? Who are we in service to? Each of us has goddesses that live inside us that help us serve here on earth, so it's a matter of who we give the mic to. For me, it's Saraswati. Saraswati works with me to help me serve at the next level! It's no coincidence that I teach about the Divine Feminine, Vedic and yogic philosophies, tools, and practices because this is Saraswati's domain. She teaches higher learning, higher wisdom, spiritual practices, classical arts, and creativity.

Saraswati's other name is Vach (voice, speaking). When I was introduced to her, I had no idea she would empower my voice and speaking. Saraswati is a vital goddess for the New Paradigm, especially as we open ourselves up to Divine Feminine Leadership because she helps us to be in flow, trust our intuition, and stay strong in our decisions.

When you are a highly creative person, you can have thousands of ideas for what you want to do and what you want to create! Saraswati will support you in choosing the one idea that would be of greatest service. It's less about thinking and more about using your intuition. You can feel this in your body, underneath your heart, between your diaphragm and rib cage. This is the true control center—not the mind. This is where Saraswati and Brahma live—in our bodies.

So, when you are passionately creative, how do you know which of your amazing ideas to choose?

You go inside and notice what is coming to the surface at that place in your body. What's top of your intuition? You listen and commit fully to that. Whether it's a Ted Talk, a book, or something to create with your family, choose your top idea, go in with 100% commitment, and watch. You choose the top, and you commit to that, and you trust your choice. Saraswati is about deep commitment. She teaches the Vedas, which is a lifelong commitment, so commitment is huge when working with Saraswati.

Perhaps you've noticed that this is where the wavering can start to happen! The mind gets involved and can take over if we let it. We start thinking, "Oh my God, I've finally chosen but did I choose correctly? Maybe I shouldn't"—a sure sign that you're stuck in your head, which means you're pretty much dead! When we're stuck in the head, we're caught up in the cycle of over-thinking and trying to figure out everything. If you're saying the words, "I'm trying to figure it out" or "I'm figuring it out," you're probably living in your head—where your Soul Purpose becomes deadened.

When you get tangled up in over-thinking, Saraswati will help you to let go and get unstuck. Saraswati is the Goddess of rivers, and rivers flow. Anytime you're in the flow, you're listening and in trust. That's when, even if you're feeling self-doubt, you trust and flow into the next inspired action. You listen, and you trust... you keep going.

Your intuition and inner guidance will keep you moving forward with inspired actions.

You can become locked in an internal battle, unable to creatively move forward if you are continually living in your head. The EMBODY practices that I teach help you get out of that suffering and connect deeply with yourself, with Source, with God, Goddess, Universe—whatever you call it— and also with others in your life: your family, your community, your students, and your leadership.

Whether it's being an incredible mom, owning it 100%, being present with your children, not reacting, not being triggered, and losing it, or it's you stepping onto the stage and serving masses of people to find themselves. Whatever you have to offer, if you are stuck in your head, you're not going to make it very far!

We all go into our head... that's human suffering. We have been taught that it isn't okay to fully embody our emotions with our feeling body and our energetic intelligence. We were taught that mental intelligence was the only way. It's part of the way, but it's not the only way. It causes much more suffering than you may be aware of until you feel and taste an Embodied state of being.

You could be a visionary person who just dives in and goes for things, but if you're also disconnected from your body, you can miss the small steps you need to take to bring your vision into creation and into service. Yet if you use your intellect and intelligence while being in your body, you will move leaps and bounds with the integrity of what you're creating.

Saraswati is wisdom and intelligence in flow.

Embodying Saraswati in your Divine Feminine Leadership means that you get to experience what it feels like to be in your whole, pure, joyful Self; to be in touch with the freedom and self-expression that has been yearning to be at the forefront of your creativity. You are standing in your power! You are owning your power, and you are serving from that place of power with every conversation you have: with yourself, with others, with the world. It means you're having that conversation with Source, and you're connected spiritually. That's what leadership means to me: Being embodied in your connection with Source, Spirit, Goddess—with Saraswati.

Activation

Saraswati brings us back to the present moment. We get to rejuvenate through specifically designed movements that we can utilize to come into this moment.

With Saraswati, it's slow, it's sensual, and requires deep presence. She brings us into that connection of being a woman. Our birthright is to be sensual, soft, slow—not submissive. Knowing that all of the decisions we make, all the paths we take, we can walk with softness and openness instead of hardness, anger, and resentment. Having our truth at the forefront, because being connected to ourselves in deep presence is what will bring us into freedom. When we integrate this rejuvenation through movement, this is Saraswati.

Here's your invitation to stand up and have an experience of Saraswati to activate this aspect of your Divine Feminine Leadership. If it's not good for you to come into standing right now, you can also practice this from sitting. Spiraling your pelvis wherever you are and however feels right for you.

If you can come into standing, then put your feet more than hip-distance apart—just a tiny bit more than hip-distance apart—you'll have your knees bent slightly, and you're going to swing your pelvis forward and backward a few times. Breathe in here. Then bend your knees deeper and jiggle! Like the Goddess has got her hands on your waist. Open your mouth: "Ha! Ha! Ha! Ha!" (This is also a great one to do when you're having your moon—shaking out the blood!).

Now rub your hands together, feel the energy that you just opened up from your creative center. This is an Activation for Saraswati. Bring your hands together, thumbs together, and fingertips together in Yoni Mudra, making a diamond shape between your thumbs and forefingers. This is the portal for the Activation. Bring that right around your belly button, so your belly button is in the center. Unlock your knees again, bend your knees just very slightly, breathing into this center. Close your eyes in this space, and sway to make circles with your pelvis in one direction.

If you are sitting on a chair, you will be grinding that chair in one direction with your yoni, your pelvis, your hips, your sit bones—making circles. If you are standing, try exaggerating the movements. Then go the other direction. With this practice, you are dislodging any debris that has been blocking you from being in your fully open channel of creativity! Woohoo!

Go with any sound vibration that is coming through for you. Sound vibration is the most powerful vibration! It will support you in releasing the things you are not, returning home to your true self, and setting you free from the prison of the mind.

Allow yourself to see your inspired actions and next steps. This is how we create anything and everything. We see the inspired actions to take. Take a deep breath in, inhale, and exhale. And when you're ready, you can release your hands and open your eyes slowly.

Journal and Integrate

What is a project or an inner calling that you have not yet moved forward with, but are ready to commit to right now? Trust your intuition with the answers you receive.

What is the one next step you get to take to move in the direction of your intention?

Where are you feeling this in your body?

- *Saraswati* -

– Divine Feminine Aligned Journal –

Free Gift:
EMBODY MEDITATION SERIES

My gift to you: A healing four-part EMBODY meditation series, in which you'll be guided with the inner-essentials for your empowerment. You'll gain the confidence to lead with courage, live your fullest self, be intimate and connected in relationships, and start rocking your Divine Feminine purpose!

Access here >> hemalayaa.com/newsletter

Biography

HEMALAYAA mentors power-house visionary women to step into their luxurious health, beauty, radiance and their embodied purpose and magnetize their desired-life with ease.

HEMALAYAA'S SPECIALTY? Musing and mentoring badass women in up-leveling their work, relationships and purpose to make a massive positive impact in the world!

Her signature HEMA Wellness Method utilizes Ancient and Modern Technologies to feel and look beautiful, radiate your magnetic energy and fuel your purpose!

Internationally recognized transformational facilitator, Hemalayaa teaches the pillars of H.E.M.A. = Healing. Empowerment. Movement. Ayurveda; a series of practices and self-nourishment rituals to enhance your lifestyle and productivity.

Hemalayaa's magnetic energy leads all into a liberated state of being: self-empowerment, inspiration, power and purpose.

She has been featured in numerous publications such as NY Times, Origin, Yoga Journal, LA Times, and Shape, as well as on the talk shows Ellen, and The Today Show.

Learn more at **hemalayaa.com**.

Medicine Woman

by Rose Cole

I had an unusual upbringing, by any standard. As a young child, I was adopted by my aunt and uncle (an Apache Native American) after years of neglect and trauma landed me in the foster care system.

To this day, many of the people that I grew up with are still addicted to drugs and alcohol, living off of the government and food stamps, and experiencing contraction in their lives. Most of my family lives below the poverty line.

My uncle was a father to me, raising me for most of my childhood. I resented his anger and volatility when we were young. After my sister–his daughter–was killed in a car accident, he became depressed and began soul searching as he tumbled down the rabbit hole of parental grief.

His tumultuous behavior changed in my teens, when–pushed to the breaking point–he returned to his deep ancestral roots with reverence, becoming enveloped by their healing rituals and practices.

Over a number of years of steadfast devotion to his path, he achieved a state that I call "sainthood." I haven't been in the presence of another person who's achieved this state. He transformed into a holy man, before my eyes.

As he continued his shamanic work, I had the honor and privilege of attending many sacred shamanic traditions, rituals, and right-of-passage ceremonies. This proximity–coupled with the transformation I watched my uncle undergo–catalyzed, inspired, and informed my future forays into shamanic healing.

Soon, I began connecting with my own dormant gifts as I reconnected with the natural rhythm and order of mother nature as a pathway to deep healing.

By connecting to three shamanic lineages, I developed a comprehensive understanding of these ancient healing systems. Inspired by my uncle's example, I learned how to use them. Soon, I could tap into the quantum field at will to heal and transform myself exponentially.

Not long after, my uncle passed unexpectedly.

In the throes of grief, I committed myself to my practices even more. Seven years later, an indigenous medicine man in my community received divine guidance that it was my path to lead and serve in this tradition and–prompted by spirit–initiated me onto the shamanic path.

My initiation sent shock waves of anger and surprise through the patriarchal shamanic traditionalists across the country. It was akin to nominating a female priest in the Catholic church. In short, it just wasn't done.

Soon, I was contacted by men from every corner of the country who were in an uproar about me being given this right, and threatened me and my daughter's safety. I froze in fear, uncertain of the path ahead, and questioning whether I was safe to continue.

At first, it felt impossible. The threats from these men–each steeped in centuries of patriarchal tradition–overwhelmed me. I shrank in fear, wondering if I should just hide, renounce my path and walk away from it all. But, of course (as with all divine assignments), I couldn't. The calling to this path was too strong.

It took enormous strength and courage to rise above this fear and contraction. One evening, while praying on my knees, I felt myself say "Enough!" to the patriarchal stigma that surrounded me. "I will not hide. This is my divine right and path."

This moment of resolve pushed me off my knees. I declared that–come what may–I would stay true to this path and follow it as spirit compelled me to.

In solidarity with my declaration, Spirit brought four indigenous shamanic medicine men into my life almost immediately. They each backed me, recognizing what I sensed all along… this is my sacred right.

Like me, they saw the rising of the divine feminine in the world and helped me understand how challenged the masculine was by this rise, especially with the return of women to the role of spiritual leaders and shamanic healers.

They called this revelation prophecy and said that it was my path to bring these teachings forward into a new era.

The fourth of these men was part of one of the only matrilineal lineages on this path. Sensing my divine alignment with these traditions, he gifted me a branch of his church.

It is rare as snow in August for a woman to lead as I do… but it was divine guidance and providence that initiated and gave me these rights.

After this experience, it became clear that every hero and heroine's journey, no matter how challenging, share one thing in common…

When you finally find true resolve and commit to courageously walk the path revealed to you, it opens up. People magically show up to guide you, and everything you need to complete your soul's mission arrives… right on time.

My years of study—coupled with the backing of my community—culminated in the development of a unique system of shamanic healing and energy work that I then incorporated into my professional work as a spiritual counselor and healer.

Soon after, colleagues and clients began asking, "What are you doing to create such profound transformations for the people you work with?" Followed quickly by, "Will you train me?"

With spirit's guidance, I was led to share the practices and methods I'd developed for over 20 years.

Today, I lead The Shamanic Academy, where we share Universal Shamanism through the lineage I birthed–Guided Energy Medicine. We train people from around the globe in shamanic energy work and spiritual counseling, giving them profound tools for quantum healing.

I believe that in order to uplift humanity as we move into a new, higher state of human consciousness, more lightworkers and healers must embody and utilize their shamanic gifts.

There is no greater method of creating quantum healing and transformation than shamanism, which points to the natural abilities and superpowers we all have, and gives us a pathway to unlock them.

Shamanism has the power to unload twenty years of baggage in one two-hour session. That's how powerful it is.

At the heart of all shamanic traditions worldwide (paganism, druidism, Inca, etc.) are the same three tenets. They teach you how to…

Have a two-way conversation with Spirit.

Work with energy: Move energy, remove energy that's not wanted, and bring in energy that's beneficial on the physical, emotional, and spiritual levels.

Influence the quantum field of possibility to generate quantum growth, expansion, and even miracles.

But perhaps most critically, shamanism centers on the principle of rituality.

These days, I look around and sense that we are reaching a crisis point as a society. We must shift out of the distorted masculine paradigms into a new, balanced dynamic with the feminine.

Those who resist this process will find themselves overwhelmed as the earth's energetics shift into higher and higher frequencies. We must steady ourselves within the rhythm of ritual in order to create the necessary harmony in our life that allows us to pass through these changing frequencies unscathed.

One of the best ways to begin integrating the feminine and masculine personally, relationally, and societally while participating in the healing of our planetary soul… is through ritual.

Rituality is close to my heart, as this was one of the keys to my own healing and awakening. Through ritual, we celebrate life's cycles, which allows us to move smoothly through times of transition or crisis.

Imagine the simple ritual of watching the sunset or sunrise, and how you feel as you bask in the warm colors dancing across the scene before you. This small moment reminds you that no matter what happens, there is always a new day. The circle of life is never complete.

This connection to the circle of life grounds us firmly back on planet earth so that we can do our work, calm ourselves down, help others, tune into our spiritual gifts, and feel joy, happiness, and peace.

There are many ways to practice rituality. In fact, you probably do many of them without realizing it. Christmas, for instance, harkens to the shamanic Pagan tradition of Yule, which celebrates the Winter Solstice and the shortest day of the year, when our intuition is heightened and the veil is thin.

Similarly, May Day connects to Beltane, the Gaelic shamanic tradition that honors the return of warmth, the sun, and everything associated with it–pleasure, excitement, joy, and fun at the midway point between the Spring Equinox and Summer Solstice.

Rituals work at the subliminal level, enabling you to untangle and rewrite your unconscious beliefs so they don't sabotage your life unwittingly.

At one point, I used a favorite ritual to discover that I believed making money is hard. I was able to quickly release and rewrite this belief on every level of my being. Imagine! Before I released this belief, it was true. Making money was hard. But after releasing it, that all changed. Beliefs are powerful!

By learning to intentionally use ritual, you tap into one of the oldest systems of personal transformation on the planet. Rituals are at the heart of shamanism and have the power to transform our life on the quantum level.

How can you find ways to celebrate the circle of life, and integrate healing traditions and rituality into your life? Keep reading for an exercise that I think will help you.

USING RITUALITY TO HEAL, CENTER, AND SOOTHE YOUR HEART

There are rituals big and small. Some can be used to mark big pivotal moments in life, like going through a divorce. Some are everyday rituals that create rhythm and mindfulness in your daily life.

Imagine the feeling of centeredness you have as you watch the sunrise and set. It's as if your body knows that there are no endings, only transformations.

This wisdom helps you welcome life, and appreciate its cycles. Your heart remains open, and you are touched and transformed as a result.

Another way we use rituality is by honoring the changing seasons through the Equinoxes and Solstices.

For thousands of years, we've honored these cycles as powerful portals for manifestation and healing. They are times to set intentions, get clear on what we're leaving behind, and decide on what we're calling in.

Think about how you can bring more ritual into your life now. It could be as simple as bringing family or friends together to celebrate the changing season, moon phases, or cycles of your life. In fact, you may already do this.

Rituality simply calls you to incorporate reverence, appreciation and clear intention into these cycles, so that you can learn from your lessons, heal, and be ready for what the future has in store.

The true nature of life is love, and by incorporating rituality into your life, you naturally become a magnet for love in all forms, as you effortlessly flow that love back into your world.

As I love to say, "Rituality is medicine for the soul."

A SELF-LOVE RITUAL TO HELP YOU HEAL AND OPEN YOUR HEART

Step 1: Lay out a carpet, tapestry, or cloth to symbolize a safe and contained space. Keep a journal and pen nearby.

Step 2: Set up sacred objects that you connect with (crystals, a framed painting or photo, or a favorite poem).

Step 3: Spend time here in silence. As you do so, begin to notice your pulse, heartbeat, and the texture of your breath.

Step 4: Place your hands tenderly on your heart or womb space (physically or energetically).

Step 5: As you feel the warmth beneath your hands, intend that your body is filled with an immense and all-encompassing kind of love.

Step 6: Feel gratitude that you're alive, with the capacity to touch, feel, smell, and see.

Step 7: Now, pick up your journal and answer the following questions:

How can I love myself more?

How can I let myself receive more?

Why do I resist loving myself or receiving in these ways?

What would incorporating these things bring to my life as a healer, lover and human?

Step 8: Call in your Guides and let yourself feel their presence. Go into a natural conversation with them. Ask questions, tell stories, and listen. Your Guides speak through words and sensations.

Step 9: Declare out loud what stands in the way of experiencing more love in your life, and let it transmute into the Universe with your Guide's help.

Step 10: Now, declare out loud what you wish to cultivate (even if your words tremble).

Step 11: Take ownership of this new energy that you're calling in, and bask in the empowerment and joy it brings you.

Step 12: State positive affirmations that help anchor in this energy. For example, you may say, "I now open my heart courageously and lovingly. It is easy to remain open-hearted. I joyfully receive all that life offers me."

Step 13: Before you return to the present moment, declare that you or your circumstances have changed and that this is the beginning of a new way of moving through the world where self-love guides the way.

Step 14: As you close up your sacred space, take a moment to thank the energies and beings that assisted your process.

Return to this exercise anytime you'd like to open your heart and infuse your life with pure, loving energy.

– *Divine Feminine Aligned Journal* –

Journal and Integrate

How can you bring more ritual into your life?

Are you really living your divine mission here this lifetime, or do you feel like you're spinning and escaping into the shamanic realms without being grounded in your purpose? If so, what do you need to get grounded and master the 3D world? (Remember, we need to have a stable 3D reality in order to give our gifts to the world.)

Journal about your experience during the self-love ritual activation.

Medicine Woman

Free Gift

ACTIVATE YOUR 9 SHAMANIC GIFTS

A 5-page E-Guide for Lightworkers to RE-member Your Intuitive & Healing Abilities. You are wired for these profound and sacred spiritual gifts! May this e-guide spark a remembrance so hot and holy within you, back to before your natural gifts were shut down by life's conditioning.

In this FREE gift you'll discover:

- Which of the 9 Shamanic GIFTS you possess
- A profound ACTIVATION Prayer to hone your UNIQUE GIFTS
- How to USE YOUR GIFTS to become an AGENT of TRANSFORMATION
- How to Claim Your Free Private Shamanic Activation Session

It's time for us as Lightworkers to reclaim our shamanic birthright, so we can become a powerful agent of change and transformation, and uplift humanity together!

Access here >>rosecole.com/freegift

Biography

ROSE COLE is a world-renowned speaker, author, and spiritual guide with over twenty years of experience as a modern-day medicine woman. She is the minister and president of the non-profit BeautyWay In Unity, and a co-author alongside spiritual leader Deepak Chopra. Over the years, she's been featured in Forbes.com, and as a popular guest on E! and MSNBC.

Rose was adopted and raised by an indigenous medicine man, who sparked a lifelong study of shamanic ritual and healing practices. Using these modalities, she healed herself from a childhood fraught with abuse, neglect, and mental illness. Today, she teaches Rituality—a way of living coined by her that shows you how to explore each moment and find your own unique truth using nature as a gateway to healing.

She currently leads The Shamanic Academy, which helps train and certify spiritual leaders from around the world as shamanic counselors and healers.

To learn more, visit **RoseCole.com**.

Sophia

by Allison Conte

In 2012, my entire life turned upside down.

Prior to this time, I was consulting with organizations around leadership and culture, while on the side, I was teaching personal development programs around the polarity of masculine and feminine, and authentic relating. I had spent more than a decade fully immersed in the integral movement centered around the work of American philosopher, Ken Wilber.

During those days, many people told me that I carried the codes of the Divine Feminine, which I loved hearing! But truthfully, I had no real idea what that meant at the time.

Until one day, when Sophia swooped into my life.

I received a message from the Divine that I needed to move my life from Ohio to Colorado. And, in a very magical way, I was transported to a big house on a large parcel of sacred land in the mountains above Boulder.

It all happened so fast that I really didn't know what had hit me. All I knew was that my soul had called me to be there.

Soon after I moved into this house, I discovered there was a temple on the property called the StarHouse. As I spent time in the temple, I realized that I had been brought to this place for a very specific reason: The temple is dedicated to the Sacred Union of Divine Masculine and Divine Feminine, heaven and earth.

I had a deep knowing that this is why I had been called, but it took a while for the whole story to unfold...

One of the first things I understood was that it was Sophia who had summoned me.

The house and temple activated me in a profound way. I began to remember past lives in which I had lived and worked as a priestess in devotion to Sophia and my role as a spiritual leader in a lineage that has existed for millennia but is not formally recognized in today's world.

A lot of things came into clearer view during the year that I lived at the StarHouse.

WHO IS SOPHIA

Many people think of Sophia as an archetype or a goddess—the goddess of wisdom.

I relate to Sophia as the Sacred Feminine… The feminine face of God, the One Divine Source of Life.

The name Sophia can be traced to a number of different groups throughout history… most notably, the ancient Greeks and some groups of Gnostics (gnosis = direct experience or direct knowing).

The gnostic groups, who existed before the Roman Empire took control of most of Christianity in the fourth century, believed that Sophia was the Divine Mother, the Creatrix of all life on earth, and the divine partner of Christ. In Gnostic Christianity, the Christos-Sophia represents the Masculine and Feminine aspects of Universal Christ Consciousness.

In Hinduism, Sophia is known as Shakti, the consort of Shiva (who represents the Divine Masculine). In Judaism, She is known as the Shekinah. In Islam, She is Ar-Rahman, the womb-like unconditional love that births all of life.

WALKING THE PATH OF SACRED UNION

Since you're reading this book, your soul probably already knows this: To create the world that our hearts are longing for—in order to bring Heaven to Earth—we must bring the Feminine principle into Sacred Union with the Masculine principle.

In other words, we must step out of the story of separation and into wholeness.

I am devoted to Sophia because I am in service to divine wholeness.

In my professional life, over 20 years, I expressed this longing for wholeness by immersing myself in studies of Gestalt therapy, integral theory, and polarity thinking. All of these bodies of knowledge are holistic philosophies that teach us about the importance of integrating seemingly opposed values, bringing them into harmony in a way that serves life.

Although I achieved mastery-level knowledge, wrote about these frameworks in a peer-reviewed journal, and taught them to leadership consultants, for a long time, my understanding of wholeness was fairly intellectual and not fully embodied. That began to change when Sophia picked me up and moved me to the StarHouse temple.

Soon after I moved in, I met my husband. For our first date on the winter solstice in 2012, I invited him to the StarHouse temple for a ceremony. I knew that he was a Christian pastor and so I extended this invitation as a test to see how he would react. (Happy to report that he passed the test with flying colors!)

After the ceremony, he walked me home under a full moon, down a dirt path, through the trees, to the house where I had been called to live. This is where I told him about the overarching purpose of the temple: the Sacred Union of Divine Masculine and Divine Feminine, heaven and earth.

"I know I have been called here for this purpose," I said.

As he offered the first kiss, he responded, "I've been searching for the Divine Feminine in my own Christian tradition, all these years. She has been in hiding for a long time. And now, here you are."

And so… That incredible first date was a foreshadowing of what was to come. We married in 2015. And we have both dedicated our lives to Sacred Union.
In 2018, we received a call from Spirit to serve this purpose together in ministry.

Just as I never saw myself being moved from Ohio to Colorado to serve the Goddess, I never saw myself going into ministry!

But if you know anything about the Divine call, you know it's not something one takes lightly or politely declines. So, this is what we are now doing. In 2020, after I gave the interview at the Divine Feminine Summit, my husband and I launched The Sanctuary for Sacred Union.

MY JOURNEY TO EMBODIMENT

The move from knowledge to wisdom—from the head to the heart to the body—takes time.

For me, the crucible of marriage has supported me to bring Sacred Union from an intellectual construct into embodied wisdom.

My husband and I are both deeply trained in shadow work. And so, of course, it came up pretty quickly after we met that we would need to do some really intensive couples shadow work together. This was some of the best inner work that I've done in my life. It has made all the difference for us as a married couple and for me as an individual.

More recently, we've been doing even deeper work to bring our soul essences together in Sacred Union. This means that our souls (not just our human vessels) are now committed to each other, beyond this particular lifetime—and we are committed to practicing, enacting, and embodying sacred union, for as long as it takes.

I believe that this is the level of commitment required if we are to help humanity rise above patriarchy and find our way to harmony with all of life.

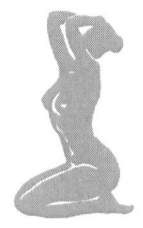

WHAT WILL IT TAKE TO DISMANTLE PATRIARCHY?

There is still so much to be done to dismantle the patriarchal culture and the structures that patriarchy created. The Feminine will preside over the destruction and the re-birth of a new world—and as Her devotees, we are called to lead the way as part of that Great Turning.

But here is the paradoxical truth: This can only happen if we turn toward the Masculine in love.

Many years ago, I had a mystical experience that showed me what it will take for us to birth this new world.

At the time, I was feeling upset with a dear friend who held the Masculine pole in our relationship. I found myself deep in complaint, criticism, and collapse, which is what the Feminine does in its shadow expression.

In this mystical experience, I was taken all the way down into the underworld. As I looked around, I saw my masculine partner (the friend I was upset with)... But he was completely dismembered. His parts were spread all over the place in the underworld.

In that moment, my heart cracked wide open. Suddenly, instead of being mad, or hurt, or in complaint... my heart opened to him. Next, I started gathering up the pieces of his body and put them back together.

Once he was whole again, we joined hands and rose up, out of the shadows, into the light.

What stands out to me about this vision is this: It was the opening of my heart and the joining of our hands that allowed us to emerge from the pain, suffering, and shadow of the underworld. The only way that we were able to rise... was to rise together.

I believe this is an important symbolic vision for what's needed in our world. The Masculine and the Feminine have both been in shadow for millennia. In the patriarchy, it's not just the toxic masculine that needs to be healed and transformed. The Feminine needs it, too.

And so as the Feminine rises, let us remember this: If we want to dismantle the patriarchy and preside over the healing and wholing of humanity, we cannot do it from a place of separation from, or judgment of, the Masculine. We will not find our way to the light or to the new paradigm from a state of separation.

We can only get there through Sacred Union, opening our hearts to and holding hands with the Masculine (both inside of us and outside of us). Only then will we come back up into the light, together, as a unified whole.

Sophia's wisdom is needed now, more than ever.

Feminine wisdom is often the opposite of what most people think of as wisdom. Paradoxically, it is sourced in values such as:

    Not-knowing
    Surrender
    Connection
    Trust
    Receptivity
    The unseen subtle realm

All of these things stand in radical opposition to how most people tend to think about wisdom. And not only that, the patriarchy would have us believe that they are signs of weakness, too.

And yet...

The most exquisite, trusting, receptive surrender to the unknown comes from the strongest sense of sovereignty. To truly surrender to something bigger than yourself, you have to stand in sovereignty and make a free-will choice. It is a generative, life-giving act.

And when we do this, wisdom flows through.

HOW MIGHT WE BRING SOPHIA'S WISDOM INTO LEADERSHIP?

One beautiful thing that is happening in my field of organizational and leadership development is the trend toward the Feminine principle. We're moving toward balancing cognitive intelligence with emotional intelligence, evaluative thinking with appreciative thinking, competition with collaboration. There's a lot of talk about creativity. There is a new focus on the value of relational leadership, perspective-taking, emergence, adaptability, and relationship.

All of these values are Feminine values. So we are heading in the right direction.

And so much more is needed.

I believe we need to go further in feminine leadership toward a particular kind of Feminine courage—I'm going to call it fire—that is fueled by compassion and connection to all of life. This kind of Feminine fire is so completely free and untethered to the patriarchy that it is unafraid to stand outside of cultural norms. It holds a torch of truth that burns through lies, deception, distortion, and distraction. It holds up a mirror to reflect all the ways that our culture is not life-giving.

The fiery Feminine says, "Stop right there. That is enough. You will not rape that mountain or cut that old-growth forest to line your greedy pockets with cash. You will not put children in cages to win the votes of people who do not care about life. I will not allow it."

Courage is the inter-dependent value that goes with surrender. We must have both.

This is Sacred Union, in action. Christos-Sophia embodied.

- Sophia -

Activation

I invite you to light a candle and enter into a prayerful/ meditative way of being.

Take a few deep breaths in and out.

Pay attention to the ground, the floor, and the seat that you're sitting in.

Relax into the earth's gravity. Give your weight over to it. Allow yourself to be held.

And now, listen through your heart.

The following words were channeled from Sophia in December 2019 for the Divine Feminine Summit.

Sophia Speaks
Wisdom is available to those who
do not look outside themselves for answers.
Wisdom is within.

You must clear the cobwebs of your understanding.
Focus on meeting me in the hall of wisdom.
Prepare yourself in this way:

Sit each morning with a candle.
Open your heart.
Offer your humble request to know.

And then consider your ability to know as infantile.
You do not know.
Ask me for guidance.

Listen for my breath, breathing you.
Listen for my heartbeat within your heart.
Listen for the rush of blood in your veins that I am moving for you.
Listen for the swirl of light passing through each strand of your DNA,
which I have given you... that you may have life.

Listen to me.

Do not worry or be afraid
or think that you have to do it all yourself.

Time will provide the answers you seek.
Stay here with me, in this moment.
Here, and now.
Stay here, with me.

Breathe. Open your mind and your heart
to receive answers that may surprise you.
Wisdom arises from surrender.

Prayer to Sophia
(from *The Sophia Code* by Kaia Ra, 2016)

"*Divine Mother of All life,*
take me to that place deep within your womb
where I can know no-thing… and be reborn."

Journal and Integrate

Which aspects of Sophia's wisdom are strong in me? Which ones need to be developed?

How might I leverage the polarity of surrender and courage in my work and life?

– Divine Feminine Aligned Journal –

Free Gift

SPIRITUAL SOVEREIGNTY

Access here >> vimeo.com/734191160/a26daf7ea1

Biography

ALLISON CONTE is a Sophia lineage priestess (since 2013), spiritual guide, leadership instructor, consultant, executive coach, facilitator, author, and speaker.

As the founder of Sophia Leadership Mystery School, Allison is committed to ushering in a new paradigm of peace, equality and environmental guardianship by developing and resourcing the women who will lead the way. Her approach unleashes the potential of women change-makers so they can deliver on their mission with impact, alignment, joy and ease. It is both a professional development program, and a spiritual journey with the Sacred Feminine.

As co-founder of the Sanctuary for Sacred Union, Allison works with her Christian-pastor husband as a guide for those on the spiritual path who are working toward Sacred Union of Divine Feminine with Divine Masculine. Their podcast, Pastor & Priestess, is available on all podcast platforms.

In addition, Allison serves as an instructor of executive leadership programs at Harvard Business School and consults with organizations around leadership and organization development.

Allison practices in the Apache Moonwalker lineage under her mentor, La'ne Sa'an Moonwalker. Other mentors include Trevor Hart, Lynda Caesara, Sofia Diaz, Barry Johnson, and Ken Wilber.

Learn more at **sophia-leadership.com** and **sanctuaryforsacredunion.org**.

Dancing with Durga

by Dana Damara

Durga is the Warrior Goddess, cosmic protector, and empowering Mother. She is the Goddess that takes us through difficulties with justice and right action at the forefront of her gaze. She is, in one moment, the gentlest, and in the next, most fierce.

She is the intense Warrior Mother who fights for liberation, truth, righteousness, and love. No wonder I felt called to get a tattoo on my arm the day after I left my marriage! The tattoo, written in Sanskrit, reads "truth, freedom, love," and I look at it every day. It was my true North as I navigated a new life as a single momma.

However, Durga entered my life subtly months before that moment.

She was with me while I was still married, grocery shopping at Whole Foods, purchasing gift cards, so my then-husband didn't know I was "saving for a rainy day." She helped me secure clients via my yoga teaching when I was unsure of my abilities. And she supported me in knowing how to parent my two young girls while stashing money away for that "rainy day."

I was filled with solid authority and potency that carried me through moving into my own home, opening a yoga studio, creating my yoga training program, and traveling to other cities to share my passion at conferences, studios, and yoga festivals.

All this before we were formally introduced.

I had no idea who she was or how powerful our relationship would become over the next ten years. But she was my guide, my protector, and she stood by me during some challenging times in my life as I raised my two daughters (now teens) on my own.

Durga is powerful because she removes the negative energies that don't serve us, those energies within, as well as those directed towards us. But she also gives us the courage to elevate our awareness and consciousness to overcome obstacles in our lives. Courage became a crucial aspect of my embodiment of Durga, as I was challenged often by internal negative forces that showed up as:

- Power struggles with an ex-husband
- Illusions of lack
- Internal battles around self-worth
- Family and societal beliefs that didn't resonate

Durga taught me to work through these challenges with fierce compassion, empowering grace, and unwavering devotion to love. She is depicted as having eight arms that suggest she protects her devotees from all directions. Her three eyes see and know all: Her left eye represents desire (the

Moon), the right eye signifies action (the Sun), and the central eye, knowledge (fire).

In the Hindu religion, Durga is believed to be the power behind creating, preserving, and destroying the world.

Durga was integral in the evolution of my devotion to the Divine Feminine when I decided to leave the marriage after eleven years and relocate my daughters and me to San Francisco, California.

Durga first visited me at a yoga festival in Squaw Valley, California. It was the first time I had presented at a festival, and I had just gained full custody of my two daughters. She showed up as a 25 lb. "murti," or statue, that I could place on my altar. At the time, I had no money for such an extravagant purchase, but somehow it worked out. I remember strapping her into the car and driving home to San Francisco with two sleeping girls in the back seat, knowing that everything would be okay.

Every day I learned more about her: I read books, listened to podcasts, and chanted her name Om Dum Durga Yei Namah—108 times, without fail. Durga is the consort to Lord Shiva, and I later learned that he actually needed her in order to exercise his power.

She revisited me one early morning before dawn—in a lucid dream. Black smoke filled my consciousness, I felt a deep heaviness on my chest and experienced an inability to move from my bed... until I pushed past it, sat up, and saw her eyes. She was staring at me with all three of her eyes, and I knew she meant business.

I had a job to do, raising these two girls and staying true to my own heart and soul's purpose.

That was nine years ago; it seems like a lifetime and yet, just the blink of an eye. I currently reside in Cardiff-by-the-Sea, California, surrounded by beauty, peace, harmony, and love. My daughters are 16 and 18 now—not quite grown but very much filled with the power of the Goddess. Durga no longer lives on my altar as I do not need to battle anymore. She served her purpose and carried me when I thought I didn't have the strength. She was my voice in many courtroom battles. She was my shield when I felt depleted. She now protects us all from the altar at the front door, along with Ganesh and Tara.

The attributes of Durga empowered grace, fierce compassion, and unwavering devotion are vital as a woman in this world right now, especially if you are embarking on a transformative time in your life. And from where I am seated, the world is shifting rapidly with no turning back. Mother Earth herself is embarking on a transformative time of reinvention like we have never seen before.

We are moving globally toward the Divine Feminine.

This energy of Shakti is alive and well, and she is armed with fierce compassion as we create a new world and new way of being. We needn't dance around a fire puja, in white robes, with flowers dripping from our hair. Nor do we even NEED to gather if we are physically unable. We just need to call on her. We must show up with courage and love, all wrapped up into one breath. We can be the mother, the teacher, the student, or the executive and KNOW that we are infused with the power of the Divine. She will never leave us, and she will always support us.

To all of you who question your abilities and are afraid to stand in who you are, you must call on Goddess Durga. She is Queenly, filled with regal radiance, fierce, and merciless. She is the one that will carry you beyond your wildest inhibitions and greet you at the gate of peace, liberation, and love to say, "Job well done."

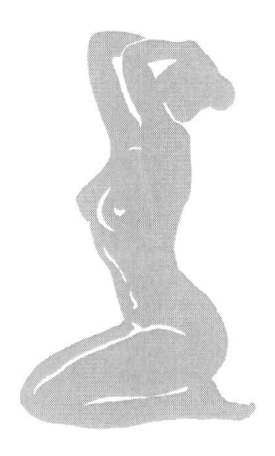

*"If there is to be a future,
it will wear a crown of feminine design."*

—Aurobindo Ghose

Journal and Integrate

When you want to call on Durga, ask yourself these questions:

What am I most afraid of? Where in my life do I need support? What have I been working on for so long, and still cannot gain traction? What can I do on a daily basis to give myself more compassion?

Where in my life do I feel depleted? As in, those places where I've tried everything I can think of to get ahead, get over, around, or gain accomplishment?

Envision yourself handing it to HER. Ask her for guidance, protection, and wisdom, and then surrender.

Where is your resistance around receiving support? What do you keep pushing and struggling against rather than surrendering to?

– Dancing with Durga –

Free Gift

DEITIES AND GODDESS ONLINE WORKSHOP

(VALUE $111, YOURS FOR FREE! OFFER EXPIRES AUGUST 15TH 2022. COURSE IS YOURS TO KEEP BUT YOU MUST ORDER/SIGN IN BY 8/15/2022)

Explore the energy of 5 of the most powerful goddesses from the comfort of your own home! Each Goddess holds healing and transformative energy that each of us embodies on one level or another. Learn how to embrace the qualities of the Goddess in your everyday living. Explore the likes of Kali, Durga, Lakshmi, Saravasti, and Parvati. Learn mantras and energies that can invoke their power into your daily life, as well as mystical priestess technologies like yoga asana, pranayama, meditation and chanting to invoke the Goddess within.

Access here >> www.danadamara.com/deities-and-goddesses

Biography

DANA DAMARA is a Master Teacher, Shamanic Healer, and astrologist based out of southern California. She began her yoga journey working with prenatal women, new mothers, children, teens, the elderly, and individuals recovering from injury and mental health issues almost 20 years ago.

Dana is a published author, Reiki Master, and entrepreneur. She has been a studio owner, wrote a 200/500 hour Yoga Training program that she continues to share each year, and has been blessed to lead workshops, trainings, and retreats worldwide. She wrote a program called Youth and Girls Elevate when her children were younger—hoping to bring yoga and mindfulness to the public school system.

She is an activist for women of all ages, offering programs that support: feminine embodiment, self-love, sisterhood, sacred ceremony, ritual, and a space for growth and evolution of your soul. When Dana Damara enters your life, everything shifts. Her power as a leader and dynamic agent of change becomes apparent when you read her books, watch her videos, or sit with her in session. Her essence is scented with truth and the leadership that naturally emerges from experience. She has an organic ability to tap into the intuitive elemental connection to women's magic and power.

As a global leader of deep wisdom and powerful ritual, she traverses the planet, offering her wealth of knowledge and breadth of understanding through private coaching sessions, global training, and a deeply spiritual and physically rigorous vinyasa practice available to everyone.

Website: danadamara.com
Instagram: instagram.com/danadamaraevolution
Facebook: facebook.com/danadamaraevolution
Podcast: soulmedicine.live
Astrological Insight on YouTube

The Sacred Courtesan

by Dr. Saida Désilets

The Sacred Courtesan is a powerful, intelligent, resourceful, and influential woman who values pleasure for pleasure's sake and who is well versed in all the arts that evoke beauty. She elegantly, and with subtle, yet potent influence, creates change in the world.

This particular energy has informed me in every aspect of my life. On a personal, evolutionary journey, she has reminded me of my worth and of the importance of experiencing and self-generating pleasure daily. Through having a strong pleasure practice, I've enhanced my mental health, emotional wellbeing, and capacity for pleasure and orgasm.

On a relational level, she's reminded me to remain sovereign in my body and desire and has shown me how to make offering of my own 'gourmet plate.' The gourmet plate is the richness of being that comes from valuing ourselves. It is the sum total of all our inherent gifts and is in contrast with the societal behavior of being a 'beggar' in relationships: where one needs the other to turn them on, to pleasure them, to fulfill them, etc.

And on the level of life contribution and business, she has taught me the Feminine way of leadership and the value of fun and pleasure in keeping my team connected and productive, while also showing me that when I'm predominantly in pleasure and relaxation, I can release the need to 'push' to make things happen. Instead, I align myself with what is actually happening in the marketplace, much like a surfer who aligns herself with a wave and allows it to carry her forward, with very little 'pushing' needed.

The Sacred Courtesan is a crucial element for moving us into a new paradigm of embodied leadership. She uses her body and senses to generate a felt-state, which is then transmitted as she speaks, for example. It is her body language and how she moves that touches those who listen, far more than her actual words, although she also skillfully and poetically uses words to encourage creativity, inspiration, and enthusiasm.

Her presence is enlivening as she holds herself with the deepest respect, while also honoring her sensuality and sexuality since she understands those qualities to be magnetic and creative. She allows for the incoherent split of separating one's body and pleasure from productivity and success to be rectified. In a way, her presence in our lives helps us build the bridge back into integrating the entirety of who we are, into everything we create and experience.

She ignites within us our birthright of sexual sovereignty, encouraging us to have a full reclamation of the right to our body, sexuality, and the space around our body, and encourages us to be responsible with this right. That is, exercising our 'ability to respond' when it comes to taking a stand for ourselves, especially our most intimate self. This means we must learn how to override our conditioning to be agreeable no matter what is happening and to be disagreeable if and when the boundaries of our sovereign space are disrespected. So, although the Sacred Courtesan's main current is pleasure, she is not afraid to exercise her authority over her own domain in order to preserve her integrity.

Another important initiation, one that directly impacts our power and ability to create in the world, is her invitation to release our addiction to woundology and victimhood. This is not an easy task when the majority utilize these aspects as a means to propagate their social justice actions. The Sacred Courtesan asks us to acknowledge that being victimized is actually a part of human life; however, it was never intended to be a part of our identity. She invites us to go deeper with our self-reclamation and healing, to seek out our deepest pain, feel it, fully embrace its presence, and sit with it until it reveals the hidden gem within it. Therefore, our greatest wound can become our greatest point of power when we choose to turn our attention to it, recognizing that it is there, yet it does not hold the power to become our identity as we move forward. The keyword here is 'identity': where we choose to assign our personal power is what we naturally become.

The Sacred Courtesan, in her deep alignment with pleasure, asks of us: "Who are we if we are not our wound? What hidden beauty lies within us? And are we willing to align ourselves with our inherent genius rather than our pain?" She knows that activation can arise when we transform our greatest pain into our greatest power. The amount of life force or aliveness that is ignited is immeasurable, and we become the unstoppable force of nature we were born to be. It is the moment we no longer need to use shame to make sure we make 'good' decisions or 'stay safe'. Rather, we start to understand that through being more sensual, more embodied, and more connected with ourselves, we will have more information to make better choices with. Through openly sharing about shame, it loses its power, and then our shameless beauty and power have the freedom to blossom.

The Sacred Courtesan orients herself to life-giving choices that align with how she perceives and thinks, how she senses and feels, and how she experiences her body's messages. She understands her responsibility when it comes to sexual tension, knowing that she is not responsible for another person's arousal, only her own. That means she can delight in sexual tension and graciously decline an invitation in such a way that the other feels seen and respected. She knows that she does not owe anyone anything, therefore, she only gives when she desires to give, and doesn't when she doesn't. This allows her to remain in integrity with herself, and deepens her self-respect and, therefore, her influence in the world. This is done through her skillful way of receiving and establishing boundaries. The receiving means she allows herself to accept the invitations that come her way, the boundaries mean that she utilizes her genuine yes and no as clear boundaries. This behavior is crucial if we are to overcome our people-pleasing conditioning. People-pleasers inadvertently make disrespectful choices when they go against their true desires in order to keep the peace: subconsciously, we are saying, "I really don't want to spend time with you, but I will so that you will be pacified."

If we desire to shift the world from a dominance-over to a harmonious, non-hierarchical way of relating, we must learn how to follow our pleasure, our yes. And if it's not a yes, we must learn to articulate our no.

The Sacred Courtesan is aware of the influence of the mother archetype and knows the detrimental impact of being a mother to a lover. Therefore, she consciously releases any mothering tendencies and cultivates more of the lover-orientation: where both people are on equal ground, where there is not an expectation of being available at all times, where there is mutual respect and there are healthy, dynamic boundaries. This is why she prioritizes her relationship with herself, making sure that she is honoring herself, wooing herself, adoring herself, basically ensuring that her own gourmet plate is overflowing with bounty. This type of practice will also buffer her from the seductive dynamics of the narcissist/empath entanglement.

She deeply reveres pleasure, not just as an immediate joy, but moreover because she understands the depth of impact pleasure has on our wellbeing. To experience pleasure, we need to have access to our parasympathetic system, the part of us that rests, digests, and has sex. It is the part that helps us rejuvenate and restore ourselves anew. Every system in our body functions more optimally when we cultivate a robust parasympathetic system. The Sacred Courtesan knows that sleep is not the only viable option. She intentionally creates and takes pleasure in beauty, allowing all of her senses to accentuate the experience of a sight, sound, taste, smell, or touch. Once she feels the initial activation of pleasure, she breathes it in, allowing her body to respond, sometimes to the point of orgasm.

Essentially, the Sacred Courtesan lives in all of us. She has been highly misunderstood, scorned, and defamed as the whore. Yet how can pleasure, devoted to integrity, truth, and an impeccable relationship with oneself, others, and life be a degrading choice? We have kept her suppressed for far too long and it is time that the elegance and the intelligence of this exquisite archetype be integrated into our psyches. When we choose to claim this essential part of ourselves, she will no longer come out sideways. We'll be more alive, robust, and centered in our power as a result. Pleasure is not frivolous, it is one of the most potent forces we can harness as we step into the most expressed and integrated versions of ourselves.

Activation

We begin with a full-body shake. The shake is important as it helps to reset the 'bio-computer'. Start with your hands & shake them out until you feel like they are made of rubber! Then shake up to your elbows and shoulders. Then shake out one leg, starting at the foot and ankle, and come up slowly to your knee, thigh and hip joint. Be sure to do both sides. Next, continue to shake out your booty and then your entire spine. If you are very stressed or experience something unpleasant, shaking will be your quickest way to support your nervous system in processing the stress successfully.

Then we will find our power pelvis stance (aka neutral pelvis). We do this by standing with feet hip-width apart and placing our fingers onto our pubic bone and also onto our tailbone. Then, see if you can line up your hands. Often one can be higher than the other. This will support pelvic and sexual health through supporting circulation and proper alignment.

Pelvic Rock: Now move your hips forward and back. You will notice that your pelvic floor/vagina squeeze when you move forward and open or relax when you move back. Have your hands resting over the lowest part of your lower belly. Do nine breaths forward and back, then inhale with neutral pelvis, squeeze your pelvic floor, and hold the breath for a moment. Release the breath slowly and notice any sensations as you breathe normally for a few breaths. Repeat as desired.

Heart/Genital Meditation: This is done seated or lying down. Place one hand on your heart and one hand on your lower belly or your genitals. Inhale to the heart and sigh 'haaaahhhh' as you exhale. After three or more breaths, inhale to your heart, then exhale down to your genitals. Imagine smiling into your heart and connecting with the feeling of heat, respect, or appreciation. As you exhale to the genitals, imagine that heat or respect flowing down and wrapping around the genitals. Then relax in this position, noticing the connection between the heart and genitals. Notice any sensations or feelings that arise.

Yoni Breathing: *Cup your genitals and as you inhale, gently expand your pelvic floor and feel like your vagina is opening. As you exhale, imagine gently squeezing the pelvic floor and vagina. Repeat three to nine times. If you are comfortable, you can add a pelvic rock, as you inhale, arch your back, opening the vagina. As you exhale, tuck your tailbone forward and squeeze your vagina gently. Repeat three to nine times. Then rest and completely relax. As you relax, start to be aware of the sensation of having your warm hand resting over the genitals. See if you can be aware of the heat of the hand moving deeper into the vulva. As you breathe slowly in and out, imagine the vulva reaching for the warmth. Finish with very light taps of the vulva, relax, and notice how you feel in your genitals and your whole body.*

Journal and Integrate

What does it mean to you to embody your Sacred Courtesan? Have one concrete example of what that looks like in your life. For example: I notice more pleasure when I'm at work and I smile inwardly at my own secret.

As you deepen your connection with your heart and genitals through the breathing practices, what is the most obvious thought or feeling that comes up for you? If it is something challenging, are you willing to simply hold yourself gently and breathe through the feelings and/or sensations?

Free Gift

THE DESIRE BOOK CLUB

For those who desire to investigate desire more deeply, I have a FREE book club that offers 13 videos, some audio meditations, and a playbook to support your exploration and the embodiment of your pleasure and desire.

NOTE: You do not need the book to participate in the videos and meditations.

Access here >> DesireTheBook.club

Biography

DR. SAIDA DÉSILETS wants to live in a world filled with audacious, sexually sovereign people, living life on their own terms.

As a counter-culture creatrix and body-philosopher, she's published *The Emergence of the Sensual Woman* and *Desire*. Her innovative method has been featured in Dr. Christiane Northrup's and Dr. Rachel Abrams' best-selling books and is at the foundation of breakthrough research in the field of Female Medicine.

Saida is renowned for being the founder of the modern Jade Egg movement and visionary spokesperson for Sexual Sovereignty, and has created eight online courses to support women into great embodiment while also hosting The Daring Project—a growing online membership of women from around the world—assisting women to audaciously move from being a victim to confidently thriving in life.

When she's not dancing, you can find Saida leading Wilderness Safaris for women in South Africa or writing deliciously sensual poetry.

Gaia

by Clare DuBois

If ever there was a time to fall into the nature of our bodies and tap the vast wisdom of the living world within us, it's now.

There is a way to open to an archetype that lives vividly in every cell of your body. There is a way to perceive both your body and the body of this planet as conduits of cosmic creativity and personal invitations to a lifetime of unabashed creative expression, pleasure, and becoming. It starts with opening your mind beyond anything you think you know to make yourself available for something greater. When you allow yourself to become a mystery to yourself, when you drop the stories of what you think you know about who you really are, something else is given space to rise inside and inform you. Dropping the stories you tell yourself may be one of the most powerful gateways you hold to the delivery of your true Self.

While intimately held by our planetary Mother, Gaia swims in space. She is dancing her rhythmic spiral dance around the central sun, in a solar system spinning through a limitless cosmos. Her song is an ancient hum that harmonizes with the songs of the other spheres, the planets that accompany her spiral dance. Gaia's intelligence is not limited by her physical form, just as our energies are not limited to our physical bodies. Her rocks and rivers, mountains and forests, oceans, and all the creatures she births into being are also singing their timeless songs and communing with each other and the stars.

Space is the apparent nothingness out of which everything arises, out of which Gaia arises, out of which all of life emerges. It is filled to brimming with an invisible tapestry of intimately relational threads of potential, including yours. Energy is dreaming itself into manifestation. The cosmos is rebirthing herself moment to moment and breath by breath, invoking the miraculous new and the endless embodiment of emergence.

It is said that the whales and the trees sing to the stars. It is said that every species of tree relates to a different planet in the solar system. It is said that the mighty Redwood and Sequoia trees are receivers of massive downloads of cosmic energy—literally uploading higher frequencies into the mainframe of life and that the whales are the only other species with sufficient mass to do the same. It is known that the whales and the Sequoias sing to each other.

What happens to us humans when we open our awareness to include the possibility of a miraculously interconnected world that is conscious and intimately relating with aspects of itself in ways that most of us are entirely unaware of? Does it touch a longing in us? Does it open up a gateway of possibility for something more? Does it show us to ourselves in a way that aches, or does it bow us to our knees in recognition of an all-encompassing blessing that is still, even now, waiting for us to wake up and join the party?

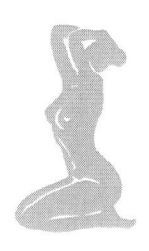

MY STORY

Gaia, infinitely creative and infinitely generous. Weaver of abundance and plenty, artist of exquisite precision and beauty, carver of canyons, sculptor of orchids, dreamer of hummingbirds and bears, paw prints, leaping Salmon, dragonflies, and cobwebs. Deliverer of deserts, mother of magma, harbinger of hurricanes, and quaker of earth. Your voice is the song of ocean waves, of wolf packs and coyote, of songbirds and eagles, of bees, blizzards, and crickets.

You sang humans into being. As you sang the trees, the rivers, and the mountains into form, as the clouds sing to the grasslands, and the wind sings to the sea. You wove us out of earth, breath and fire, rain, rock, stardust, and the promise of intimacy. You wove us out of a dream of discovering a path to wholeness through union with all things. You showed us how the trees tend each other, how the soils are living highways of communion and unconditional love. You showed us how no tree stands alone, how we are all intimately connected by invisible threads of starlight and longing, of the need to create and birth and die, to be delivered again into oneness with all things in the ocean of endless time.

Gaia—mother of everything we know and don't know. Creator of everything we need and everything we love. You have taught us what beauty is, what giving means, what reciprocity could be. You have shown us what a human could be if we could respect the sacredness of every living thing. (After all, the DNA of every living thing in this world exists within our own so-called 'junk' DNA) We are it all. We are you, inseparable, universal, destined to remember who and what we are as a facet of your brilliance. May we find our way home through the gateway of humility and intimacy into a belonging so deep that the very purpose of our existence becomes the regeneration and nurturance of your every thread of creation. Thank you.

THE COSMIC PELVIS:
A Centering and Expansion Practice of Enhanced Perceptivity

This is a deeply intimate and deeply effective practice for shifting your state in an instant. It draws your attention to your tailbone as one might stir a cauldron into a rhythmic, spiraling, meditative state. The focus of micro-movements requires engagement with all the muscles of the pelvic floor and beyond. Hence, it draws your attention down to the creative source of the female body where we centre awareness in the creative cauldron (your womb—whether you have a physical womb or not, the energetic womb remains perfect and intact) that contains the cosmos.

First, you may want to shake your body as fervently and completely as needed to allow your whole self to start ringing. Shake until you laugh, roar or cry. That is not a half-hearted activity, and you could benefit from some really good music! If you can follow on with some sublime, languid, flowing, endless transient music for pelvic rotations, even better.

Having shaken, find yourself a quiet place where you can sit either cross-legged or on your knees, comfortably enough so that you know you can rotate your pelvis.

Start with your breath, finding your intimacy with the sensations of both in and out-breath. Notice whether you can find it luxurious, flowing, and easeful. Do not force anything, do not try to change anything. Just notice whether you can find pleasure in your breath.

As your breath moves through your body, lower your attention to your pelvis and your tailbone. The invitation is to start spiraling your tailbone clockwise in the tiniest circles, possibly less than half an inch in diameter. It may feel achingly small, but with all your attention placed at that fulcrum of your central axis, half of that circle can take your inner breath and half an out-breath. The minute movements can feel immense. The closer you pay attention to the muscles required to move so simply and fluidly, the more your energy moves down into the pelvic bowl.

As you start to find the spiral of your pelvis, begin to imagine that your tailbone is gliding through the night sky. That tiny intimate circle is cruising through the vastness of the cosmos, a planet in your inner solar system rotating around a central sun. Allow your awareness to expand to include the feeling of immensity holding your whole body in space. Know that these vast cycles of your tailbone are literally stirring the energy of our galaxy and allowing every cell in your body to start imbibing vastness.

Whether you have a physical womb or not, you have a creative reservoir within you that is ruled by the moon, which receives a cosmic spark and creates life. As you breathe, as you spiral and build energy in your pelvis, you can consciously breathe immensity into your womb space. You can literally become pregnant with possibility. You are becoming a living invitation for creativity, and into that creative space, you can place your questions.

Part of the meditation is to draw that vastness of space in through every surface of your body, not just into your pelvic bowl but with the awareness that the space inside every cell of your being is vast enough to hold the cosmos. This is a process of both stirring and drinking limitlessness. It's a form of soul hydration, of plugging ourselves back into the vastness of creation that is flooded with an intelligence available to us in every moment that we open our awareness to connect with it. It's a way of becoming porous to a greater intelligence and intimate with creativity itself.

Keep a journal close. Allow your whole body to begin to respond to those micro-movements in ways that magnify and mobilize your whole body in relationship to the cosmic spiral. Your arms may raise and float like wings. Your spine, fluid and snakelike, may respond with life-flowing undulations that bring pleasure and alter your state. With your attention down in your pelvic bowl, the rest of your body can simply respond to whatever begins to rise. And what can begin to rise is a different intelligence: the cosmos alive in you.

There will be a natural point at which you feel as if you are at the peak of your spiral dance, and the invitation is to place a question into your pelvic bowl or to listen for a stream of consciousness in answer to these words... 'The cosmos in me knows... what?'

If you are doing this with a friend, you can take it in turns whilst still spiraling to end that sentence verbally again and again and again, then fall into silence and listen to her doing the same thing. You can let that be a backward and forwards dance of allowing the voice of the cosmos to speak through you both. Or you can lie down with your journal and pour the fullness out onto the page using the prompts at the end of the chapter.

If you want to go deeper with this, you can oscillate between contraction and expansion as a practice. Moving between this prompt... 'I keep myself small in order to... what?' and whichever of the three prompts above most resonates with you in that moment. Then go back to your smallness, and see how both your body responses and your emotional awareness shift as you allow yourself to transition from one to the next and back again. The more we can make friends with the feelings in both places, the more we can set ourselves free to let go of what we're not and move joyfully towards the magnificence that we are.

Remember, Gaia holds nothing back. She is total in everything that she does. Whether she is stripping her leaves and falling below soil into the roots of a dreaming tree, whether she is a tornado tearing things asunder, whether she is the featherless body of a newly hatched chick, the infinite patterns of swirling snowflakes, the volcano erupting from the deep, or the serenade of whales song wrapping their coral melodies around our world, everything is given in fullness.

Gaia's invitation to each of us? To live fully and to hold nothing back. To live ecstatically, outrageously, beautifully, unpredictably, magnificently, tenderly, subtly, erotically, undeniably, generously, unconditionally, reciprocally, and with reverence and respect both for ourselves and for all other living things.

She is your living invitation to discover who and what you are as part of her body and her beingness. She is your permission, if permission is needed, to drop the need to hold back and stay small and to allow her living energies as they flood through your body to inform you about what it means to be human.

Activation

I invite you to light a candle and enter into a prayerful/ meditative way of being.

Take a few deep breaths in and out.

Pay attention to the ground, the floor, and the seat that you're sitting in.

Relax into the earth's gravity. Give your weight over to it. Allow yourself to be held.

And now, listen through your heart.

The following words were channeled from Sophia in December 2019 for the Divine Feminine Summit.

YOUR PLANETARY SELF

Let the birds take your clothes
Let the waves undo your holding back
Let the vines unravel your tired mind
And the earth savour your sweat and tears.
Let your stories burn off like rising mist,
As your past and the false floors of curbed self-love
Dissolve into butterfly wings and fireflies
As your edges blur and your Planetary Self ignites.

Let the trees bathe your breath
Let the meadows embrace you
Let the mountains and the bees remind you
Let the sky flood in and allow the clouds to guide you.
Let your undoing be as total
As your becoming is beautiful—
And when the living world has climbed inside
Enough for you to feel four legs, scales, and wings.
May you finally know yourself alive as all things—
Indivisible and responsible
Reborn into wholeness
Natural, Sacred, and Wild

—Clare Dubois

– Divine Feminine Aligned Journal –

Journal and Integrate

Lie down with your journal and pour the fullness out onto the page using these words as a prompt again and again:

The cosmos in me knows...
When I open to limitlessness...
When I become vast...

- Gaia -

– *Divine Feminine Aligned Journal* –

Free Gift

"REWILDING YOUR FEMININE NATURE"

A three-day mini-course to ignite your instinctual feminine heart.

To access, sign up for a free account here:
treesisters.org/grow-yourself/courses/rewilding-your-feminine-natu

Biography

CLARE DUBOIS is the founder and CEO of **TreeSisters.org**, a global women's movement spanning multiple countries, that has collectively funded the planting of over 18 million trees. TreeSisters is a social change movement and a tropical reforestation organization working towards normalizing cultural reciprocity with nature. The aim of both Clare and Tree-Sisters is to make it as normal to give back to nature as it currently is to take nature for granted while supporting humanity in its transition from a consumer species to a restorer species. Before founding TreeSisters, Clare worked internationally for over two decades, coaching business leaders and facilitating group behavior change processes in multiple sectors. Known for her direct, catalytic energy, her inspirational speaking, and her holistic approach to collective transformation, Clare is a walking invitation to anyone ready to step up and step in on behalf of the planet.

Athena

by Mayabello Fiennes

In 2012, my entire life turned upside down.

Prior to this time, I was consulting with organizations around leadership and culture, while on the side, I was teaching personal development programs around the polarity of masculine and feminine, and authentic relating. I had spent more than a decade fully immersed in the integral movement centered around the work of American philosopher, Ken Wilber.

During those days, a lot of people told me that I carried the codes of the Divine Feminine, which I loved hearing! But truthfully, at the time, I had no real idea what that meant.

Until one day, when Sophia swooped into my life.

I received a message from the Divine that I needed to move my life from Ohio to Colorado. And, in a very magical way, I was transported to a big house on a large parcel of sacred land in the mountains above Boulder.

It all happened so fast that I really didn't know what had hit me. All I knew was that my soul had called me to be there.

Soon after I moved into this house, I discovered there was a temple on the property called the StarHouse. As I spent time in the temple, I realized that I had been brought to this place for a very specific reason: The temple is dedicated to the Sacred Union of Divine Masculine and Divine Feminine, heaven and earth.

I had a deep knowing that this is why I had been called, but it took a while for the whole story to unfold...

One of the first things I understood was that it was Sophia who had summoned me.

The house and temple activated me in a profound way. I began to remember past lives in which I had lived and worked as a priestess in devotion to Sophia and my role as a spiritual leader in a lineage that has existed for millennia but is not formally recognized in today's world.

A lot of things came into clearer view during the year that I lived at the StarHouse.

– Athena –

EVERYBODY LOVES DANCING

KundaDance is a journey through the chakras. Each movement is seven minutes long and clears each chakra. By working with seven chakras in 49 minutes, you can receive a full, daily injection of potent energy.

KundaDance allows for serotonin, dopamine, oxytocin, and other feel-good chemicals to be released. It burns calories and helps to balance hormones in the body. The dance guides one through each chakra—clearing and cleaning. I love it because even people with no yoga experience are able to join the dance.

I was happy to notice how many people tended to laugh at the end of the dance because of the joy and silliness that was activated in them through this movement practice.

I've listened to Athena for many years and here is my take on her message:

Do whatever makes you feel good.

There is nothing more powerful than passion, so activate your passion by asking: "What makes me feel good?" Regardless of whether or not you are clear on your direction, just allow your passion to talk to you and guide you to receive clarity about what you love.

That's it. It's very simple.

LETTING GO OF SUFFERING

We have this notion that we have to work hard. We have to make everything hard. And only when it's hard will we feel the benefits and believe it works. But I believe that's an old way of thinking.

I created KindaDance because I desired to make it easier for all of us to be happier and to not have to suffer so much. Even though suffering requires that we break through the pain to get to the other side, it doesn't have to be so hard! With KundaDance, you can simply enjoy it, and you WILL feel it in your body the next day, as all your muscles have been challenged. Your mind and emotions become more clear and you begin to feel more joyful. This dance offers us a new way to live—with more ease and joy!

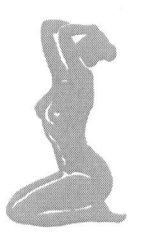

CALLING ON THE GODDESS

Athena comes to me much more strongly now than she used to. I pray and call to her every day. I call in Zeus, Athena, Aphrodite, Kira, and other gods and goddesses. I bring them into my life. I activate them by calling their names, by asking them to be with me. Because if you don't ask, the universe won't know what to deliver!

However, you have to be confident to call on the Goddess—and trust that she will show up for you. Every day, I go within and ask. Then I breathe on it and constantly reinforce it throughout the day. For example, recently, I changed my name from Maya to Mayabello. Even though my name isn't yet official on paper, my passport, or my driver's license, I use Mayabello with everyone I meet because if I don't use it and embody the energy of the new name, then the activation of this uplevel of my consciousness is not there.

I call on Aphrodite when I want to express my femininity. I sometimes will wear a dress instead of yoga pants because I want to feel good and it requires a different frequency. In order to embody the new frequency, I stopped watching the news. I am just not interested because all the news is bad news! Instead of buying into the fear, I've chosen to believe that the world is the most beautiful place and I focus my attention on positivity. In Nepal, the people have no food, but the people are still smiling. They're happy and their fourth chakra—their heart—is open. They're laughing, and they welcome you. They share whatever they have with you.

When you call on the Goddess, you cannot receive Her messages if you're not open. This is why we work every day to clear the chakras with KundaDance. Only then, the energy is flowing and your crown chakra can fully receive messages from the universe.

Your intuition comes from the sixth chakra. This is where Athena talks to you. But we have to constantly work on our body, mind, and spirit to be clear and an open channel—allowing, giving, and receiving.

Sometimes the rigidity of the mind can be a problem! So it's important to allow your mind and heart to work together. With yoga, breathwork, and mantras, the mind and the heart will align. The door to meditation is the breath, so when you activate your breathing and circulation and then chant mantras, it's much easier to sit in meditation because there is congruence between your heart and your mind. Start by just breathing for two minutes. This is the beauty of kundalini yoga—the breathing exercises can be just two minutes, but they change the whole flow of your energy and how you think. It's very beneficial!

Activation

ATHENA ACTIVATION

> *Sit down comfortably. You don't have to sit cross-legged. Let's activate a series of breaths called the immune booster. You can boost your immune system by breathing only through the left nostril, which corresponds and connects to the stimulation of the parasympathetic nervous system. We tend to always go, go, go, so that's when we can feel fatigued because we need more energy. The adrenaline is pumping and it's all too much. We just need the parasympathetic nervous system to relax—yoga and meditation is great for this.*

2-MINUTE BREATH OF FIRE PRACTICE

Start by closing the right nostril with the right index finger. You're going to breathe only through the left side. On the left hand, you're going to do a mudra with the ring finger where you usually wear the wedding ring, ring, and thumb together. You're relaxed, chin down, close your eyes, activate the third eye. You're looking In between your eyebrows and you're going to breathe, inhale, exhale, inhale, exhale, with quick, equal amounts of breath.

Now, inhale, and hold. Interlace the fingers in front of your eyes and pull like you're trying to separate your hands and you're holding the breath, hold... and then exhale. Stay for a second. Observe, receive, open, feel what's going on, meet it. You can feel the calmness. Do this for two or three minutes depending on how much time you have.

As the head and the heart move together, you may visualize whatever you want. After that, you can either slow down and just close your eyes, go into meditation, or stay up and activated while going on with your day.

As a classical musician, I loved creating music for the KundaDance mantras. I see now that was my purpose! After all those hours and hours of practicing piano and chanting mantras... I would literally put my hands on the piano, close my eyes, and use playing as meditation. I just allow my hands to move... I don't know where the music is going to go, or which chords I'm going to play. I don't know... I don't want to know, and I don't want to prepare! Sometimes it's right, sometimes it's not, but I don't care! I just completely let go. And then 10 minutes later, I open my eyes. Wow. What just happened? I'm in complete bliss from this meditation.

I remember when I was at a modeling photoshoot, the photographer was moving all around me and he was dancing with a camera as he was going around. "What are you doing?" I asked. "I'm using chi-gong and meditation while I'm taking the pictures," he shared.

They were the best pictures ever.

Similarly, KundaDance is a form of spiritual devotion. It's a dance of prayer and devotion to spirit. With KundaDance, I know that Athena is supporting me as I honor the magic of my journey and the mystery of life through the movement of my own body and soul.

Journal and Integrate

What do you love right now?

Sit quietly and ask the Wise You what she wants to tell you. Ask for guidance from the Divine feminine as you journal:

Where do you want me to be?
What do you want me to do?
Who shall I talk to and why?
What is my purpose at this stage of my life?

Free Gift

A JOURNEY THROUGH THE CHAKRAS - WISDOM

This is a guided practice to clear and open the sixth chakra. This class is a total workout to help you deal with depression and find happiness. In this class, Maya guides you through the abs and the digestive system and teaches you how to balance out the hormones and create happy hormones. You'll also learn about how to deal with happy hormones and be more decisive, clear foggy brain, stimulate the brain and deal with anti-depressive chemicals, clear nervousness, anxiety, negative and unwanted thoughts and worries about the future, and maintain a creative, neutral, judgment-free mind so that you can finally be truly happy.

Access here >> vimeo.com/242642907/2af16b9cea

Biography

MAYABELLO FIENNES is an author, yogi and musician who travels the globe teaching a mix of Kundalini yoga, Tai Chi, and Qi Gong, incorporating original music that she have written to help her students with the music written at the "healing frequencies".

Her journey from concert pianist to yogi is a confirmation that anything is possible if we allow it and believe in it!

Maya has produced over 20 DVDs and CDs and authored Yoga for Real Life, which empowers people to tap into their potential of self-healing through mindfulness and meditation. She has also developed The Maya Fiennes Method which helps her students transform their lives and find their path to freedom… from fear, anxiety, and stress. She is also the creator of Kundadance a creative movement class that works on your chakras. Maya hold regular retreats, events and teacher training courses around the world helping people unlock their potential and give them access to joy!

Warrior Goddess

by Kimberly iMfezi Ingonyama Baskett

When we look at the world around us, it's easy to see there is a leadership crisis. We see the evidence of this crisis spans across the global healthcare system to our climate.

From the East to the South, West and North we hear a clarion call for a new kind of leadership—a brand of leadership that honors, respects and elevates facts, logic and reason as much as discernment and intuition.

Leadership that is not rooted in toxic hierarchies, sexual dysfunction, victim consciousness and savior complexes.

When I think about how the world is turning, I ask myself:

Is this the world I want to live in?

Is this the world I want my children to inherit?

When I ask myself those questions, the answer is both No and Yes.

We live in a polarized Universe, so while we are faced with some very serious challenges that we ignore at our own peril, I'm keenly aware that the solution is always contained within the problem.

The good news is; we are that solution. Our courage. Our conviction. Our commitment to course correct the current trajectory. All of this is well within our control.

So I'm calling upon the warrior goddess that lies within each of us to do what must be done so that we can shape the world into one that our ancestors envisioned.

I know my ancestors didn't go through all that they went through just so our children could inherit the world in this current state.

Now is the time to elevate what it means to be a warrior and a goddess, regardless of whether or not we believe or agree that spiritual warfare is happening around us.

Across the span of space and time, I sense I've been a warrior many times over. Some of those lifetimes I've operated with a high level of integrity and others I left quite a bit of collateral damage along the way.

In this lifetime, my work is to pioneer a new consciousness of leadership rooted in synarchy; to co-create a tribe of sovereign leaders who are leading alongside other sovereign leaders.

This is the medicine that I'm honored to carry.

So how do we embody our Sovereignty? How do we bring forward all the divinely feminine resources that we were born with, such as intuition, magic, and our connection to the elements?

The power to alchemize all that is no longer serving this planet and transmute and transform it into the lived experiences we all desire?

When these traits are combined with masculine energies of intellect, strategy, and execution, the Warrior goddess activates us to look at the suppressed energy of sacred rage and use it as fuel for positive, sustainable change.

The Warrior Goddess archetypal energy in me harnesses all of nature's power… all of my experiences, those of my ancestors, and the divine co-creative power that exists in me to speak truth and create a world that I want to inhabit.

We all possess the power to create worlds.

Leadership is a sacred calling. When I say that, I feel every cell in my body vibrate, and it feels like it's no less of a calling than being in the clergy or holding the highest political office.

Many of us decided to come back into this lifetime to serve as pioneers. We knew we would land right here in the middle of such turbulence. And we came fully resourced to handle all that we will encounter.

My decision to leave corporate was a slow burn. About ten years into my 21-year corporate journey, I thought, "Okay, I can either stay here for 20 years, or I can leave now."

I was already starting to feel some disconnection and awakening to the truth that I no longer belonged there. I had a felt sense that my work, while still devoted to leadership, extended beyond the halls of Corporate America.

Yet, I didn't go right away. I stayed for many reasons: the perks were really good, and I entrained into that particular programming of what it meant to be a leader. But, I also needed that experience to have this conversation with you right now.

Nothing is wasted in the Universe. Every experience I've ever had led me to this moment in time—in divine time.

And then, Source gave me a catalytic opportunity to rethink my entire life.

I had just gotten promoted to my senior executive position, and at the same time, I was getting a divorce; the intersection of those two worlds was like a head-on collision.

I lived in Kansas City, and the company that I worked for was headquartered in Texas. I was told I had to move or be fired.

But I was about to be a single mom—I couldn't move. My daughter's father was in Kansas City and the courts required me to stay.

During this time, I was still operating from the unhealthy warrior paradigm. I felt I needed to defend myself at every turn. Everywhere I looked, I saw a potential threat. The warrior in me was fighting tooth and nail to relocate my daughter inside of a ton of pressure to do so, but ultimately, we didn't relocate.

I had been told I was going to lose my job. And I was thinking, "What? How can I lose my job? I've been dedicated to this for 12 years. My whole identity is associated with this work and with this title."

I remember finally saying to God, "Look, I'll do whatever you want, but here are my priorities. I love you. And I trust you. And my daughter is my priority. Anything else that you do? Anything else that you take? I don't care, but I'm a mother first. I'm a mother above all things."

I realized that I had, for years, been declaring my value system as 1. God; 2. Family; 3. Work. But what I was actually living was a value system of 1. Work; 2. Family; 3. and God in a pinch.

So I got realigned and served all sorts of things up to the altar. Then, slowly, I started making my way out of the company. I wish I could say that it was an elegant exit, but it wasn't because I can be hard-headed. My friends jokingly say that I "Chernobyl-ed out of there!"

Sometimes it's just hard, and that feeling that we all have... that's the Warrior Goddess energy that says, "I want what I want, I'm going to do it the way I want it."

Being a warrior goddess in these modern times requires surrender in many ways. To surrender to your higher self as well as your calling. In my experience, surrender is one the bravest things we can do.

I believe that we need powerful leaders at all levels of the business and corporate worlds and beyond. The paradigm of leadership that we all grew up in, and where I learned to be successful, is asking to be OVER.

We need a new model of Sovereign—multidimensional—Leadership.

What we need is a new model for how we're taught to lead. I have fierce compassion and for those leaders who created those organizations with a board, shareholders, constituents, clients, and multiple bosses. If you can be successful under those terms and conditions, you are indeed a warrior.

I believe we're being called to model to the world how it's safe and viable to lead from this model.

I do see a lot of evidence that people are desirous of change. A true leader wants highly empowered and engaged employees, peers, and colleagues. However, the current system doesn't have a consistent model for how to do this well.

We all have the capacity to explore which pieces of the puzzle we can bring to the table.

Many humans fear being different from the group and perhaps ending up outside of the proverbial tribal circle and getting stoned to death. Well, the truth is, that's not really going to happen.

So, what is true? What might happen if you dare to be authentic?

The willingness to ask and answer these questions for ourselves—and then take guided action—is the warrior goddess ethos.

So, how do we do this well? First, look for evidence of what is true (Leaders tend to be good at this, and Corporate America tends to love data).

Start accumulating data about what's true in the environment versus what you've read or what you fear, and then act accordingly.

Test it. Start split-testing. What happens when you show up as your most authentic self in a meeting? What happens when you don't? Make your adjustments. Change your approach; change the trajectory.

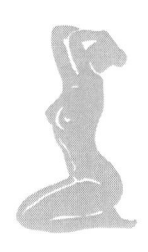

BOOTS ON THE GROUND

First, start to ritualize your day. Create a way to bring some rituals into your day and see how that shifts how you show up and how people respond to you.

Be intentional about how you start your day. So if you're starting your day

yelling at the kids or yelling at the dog, that's a ritual. Whether or not you think of it that way, you've ritualized your day to start with negativity.

DO THIS, NOT THAT

Set a ritual where you connect with the divine feminine and divine masculine energies within you every morning. In corporate jobs, we are required to bring forward a lot of masculine energy. Too often, it's less than healthy. It's the stuff of hustling, grinding, and hyper-productivity. Instead, you can choose to make a practice of being intentional about connecting with the sacred masculine. Over time you will notice a shift in your power and how you show up as a leader—from the boardroom to the bedroom.

Connect with the Divine Mind as part of your daily ritual. When you start your day by connecting in a ritual with Divine Mind and weaving this connection into your sacred feminine and sacred masculine energy, as well as your Body as Temple, then you're accessing new resources that can help you be more strategic, balanced, and measured in your approach as a leader. You're harmonizing intuition and intellect, and that formula is my super-secret weapon. Leading from this paradigm is a radical act of sovereignty.

The System is designed in a certain way, and there's an agreement that we're going to operate in a certain way to be successful within that System. The System just wants what it wants, and it's pretty ambivalent about whether or not you're going to agree to operate in agreement or not.

In this way, I like to say the System doesn't discriminate. It has no use for anyone who has the audacity to question it or work outside its limiting and prohibitive norms.

I am bringing in more fierce compassion and grace for those of us who are in that system. And for those who wake up one day thinking, "What happened to my sovereignty and my sense of freedom?"

We're trained from a very young age to seek approval outside of ourselves. It starts when we're toddlers. We go to touch something that we find attractive or beautiful and your mom comes and says, "Don't touch it. It's fragile." When we comply, we look at her and she smiles and we're like, 'Oh, okay. That's how I learn what I can and cannot do. This is what it takes to be approved of; this is what it takes to feel safe and good.' That sense of approval from an authority outside of myself feels good in my body. We begin to equate that feeling with love, and we make our decisions and choose from that place. Until we don't. Or no longer can't, because something begins to stir within us. This is the sense of our Inner Authority. Our Sovereignty.

So that happens over and over again. And it's reinforced in multiple ways and in all relationships. So when we end up in corporate America as leaders, if we're not intentional about deactivating that code of "I seek approval outside of me" or the code of, "I wait for permission before I take the next step," then that's how we're going to show up.

Again, ritualizing your day and connecting with the higher energies to alchemize what is no longer serving you, takes you one step forward to deactivate those codes and activate your sovereignty. I believe we're all born sovereign and our quest is to remember and actualize this truth.

I wrote a short post the other day about professional intimacy, and how we are being invited to step into more of it and show up more authentically. The key is your willingness to be seen.

A number one challenge for top leaders today is the veneer that they have to present the persona that they were taught to present in order to appeal or be considered successful. That is the old leadership paradigm—the imposter syndrome! It's a virus in corporate America. It is this idea that you have to pretend to be someone you are not, and it takes a toll on you.

The pandemic has, in some ways, served as an equalizer. Zoom meetings are held in make-shift offices that people have converted from their closets. There's an energy of equanimity because now we're all just in our closets. We can all just let our hair down a little bit and realize that imposter syndrome is a manmade construct. We need to stop pretending to be someone we're not, and allow ourselves to be as powerful as we TRULY are, especially powerful women.

THIS IS SYNARCHY

I'm a sovereign leader who leads alongside other sovereign leaders. And I'm very intentional about helping my team and everyone who works with me empower themselves to become sovereign because that's more fun and strategic in the long run. It allows us to execute in a way that feels future-forward. That's bringing all your divine power to the boardroom. That's a whole different way of leading in. In synarchy, everyone brings their A-game—and everyone's unique gifts and talents are recognized and celebrated.

One thing that got sacrificed in my{corporate} life, without even realizing it, was my femininity. I just didn't have the consciousness at the time to know that I had a divine feminine aspect. And so I remember the moment that I woke up and realized I'm a black female. That sounds crazy, I know yet it's true. I had been living my life from deep within a matrix that didn't have me identify as a powerful brown-skinned woman. It was the awakening of who I really was and the authenticity and the wisdom of why I came into this body. I believe we pick our body and allies to align with our divine mission, and we live in a universe that is built on polarity, so holding that tension between those two energies is not about gender. Rather, it's the energetic gateway to one's freedom.

I came in as a Black female in an ancestral lineage of enslavement because it is my divine mission to guide one million souls to sovereignty. It's taken me some time to say it out loud with truth in my body. But every cell in my body vibrates with this understanding. It's my deep honor to do this work. To be this mission.

And so I came as a Black female in this body with all of my goddess power and all of my lifetimes of experience because I am a spiritual abolitionist. In this lifetime, it's no longer about being in physical shackles. Modern-day enslavement is about our consciousness— t mental slavery, spiritual slavery, emotional slavery. My sense is I have multiple lived experiences of enslavement as well as experiences of total and complete sovereignty and divine power. This epigenetic combination informs my spiritual DNA and it's why I chose this path.

I'm here to decolonize our minds and abolish slavery in our spirits… for the benefit of all sentient beings who are now here or will be in the future.

Activation

Say each one of these affirmations nine times, out loud, to activate your throat chakra. The solar plexus is where your inner authority, or power, is stored yet it is your throat chakra where power is expressed. Saying these words aloud activates your throat and sends a vibration of truth that resonates across all realms and dimensions. This is where your fierceness comes in.

I am divine sovereign power.
I am sovereign divine femininity.
I am sovereign sacred masculinity.
I am perfect, whole, and complete.

Journal and Integrate

Journal what it means to you to be a divinely powerful sovereign being with both feminine and masculine energies.

How will you integrate and balance these divine powers in your life going forward?

– Divine Feminine Aligned Journal –

Free Gift

13 POWERFUL SACRAL CHAKRA PROMPTS

Access here >> wildfireglobal.com/resources/

Biography

KIMBERLY IMFEZI INGONYAMA BASKETT

Kimberly is the founder of Wildfire Global, a boutique leadership coaching firm for high-impact, conscious leaders and entrepreneurs. She envisions a world where a diverse slate of empowered, intuitive leaders are guiding the world's top businesses, corporations and political offices

Kimberly has mentored, advised, coached and sponsored hundreds of leaders over the years. Her clients are courageous leaders with a proven track record of success and who are committed to manifesting their big vision into the world.

After more than 20 years at a fortune seven firm where she led teams as large as 10,000 employees and managed portfolios valued at more than $14B, Kimberly traded in her golden handcuffs to put her hand at leading her own successful company period.

She's been a senior executive, married, divorced, and married again. She's been highly sought after and she's been fired. Today, Kimberly is devoted to bringing all of her experiences to the table in order to serve her clients in their quest to lead lives of financial freedom and true sovereignty.

Learn more at wildfireglobal.com.

High Priestess Edge Walker

by Anahita Joon

There was a moment in the early months of the COVID pandemic when I noticed how well I was doing. "Why am I doing so well?" I asked myself.

And then I remembered that the first eight years of my young life were spent in Iran during an Islamic revolution and war, where I experienced active bombings and the violent shaking of our home regularly. I was afraid to close my eyes because I was in constant fear of dying.

That was my childhood. And it was a gift because living in the uncertainty of wartime and food rations catalyzed me to find my certainty from an internal place. Facing so much uncertainty at such a young age (fear of life and death, fear of not having enough) has prepared me well for dealing with the covid pandemic.

Many people around me have never faced this level of uncertainty around life and death, financial stability, the market, and the government. Fortunately, I've seen my clients and community shedding what is not stable and becoming authentically aligned to what is stable. A purging of the old is taking place, and people are saying, "I'm awake. I want to move through this." But how? What is the new foundation, and how do we create a stable one amid such chaos?

First, it's important to go back to basics, starting with self-care. To be fully aligned with your feminine power requires tuning in and connecting to the frequency of your body. Right now, feel into your aliveness, vitality, health, arousal, and creativity. How much of this high frequency is available to you in your body right now? Ask yourself, "What am I creating? What am I doing? What do I need to thrive at this time?" In my experience, the way through the struggle is simply to feel it, feel it, feel it until you're no longer responding or creating from your pain-body but have transmuted the energy so that you are creating from your ecstatic body.

Recently, I was researching sex trafficking and female genital mutilation. As I landed on the images and videos, I felt a wave of overwhelm and was about to click away when suddenly I thought, "No!" So instead of turning away from the discomfort, I made myself go deeply into the feelings—especially the anger. I was so angry. After I was done being angry, I just collapsed. And then I found myself moving my body back and forth for a few hours, weaving in this new sensation and processing my feelings. Afterward, I needed to declare it so I posted on Facebook, "Who's standing with me? We get to do something! But not without feeling it—because as long as we're not feeling or moving forward without feeling it, we won't be able to create the impact we desire."

It's powerful to allow your feelings to wash through and over as you get clear, and then you can create from commitment rather than from stuckness or pain. There's so much that needs our love, compassion, and attention these days. We can easily slip into "rescuing mode," but all women are powerful creators at the end of the day—no one is the victim of their creation. It's a healing journey that allows us to arrive at that deep knowing of our power.

I've noticed that sometimes change doesn't move as fast as I'd like it to and that there are two parts of me at play here: the younger, more immature part of me that marched in the streets and who was so angry for being oppressed for so long, who wants to do something. And then there's the wiser, more mature, slightly-more-tired-and-weathered part of me who gets to keep feeling this but then asks herself, "What is mine to do?" As I practice asking myself this, my vision gets bigger and includes other people. It's not about me being the rescuer. It's not about me expressing my outrage at the injustice. It is about how I can authentically say, "I've really felt this; now let's create something different."

Let's look at two archetypes. First, there's the High Priestess. She is the line anchoring in the divine feminine consciousness. She lives a sacred life and reaches a deep level of devotion and mastery that allows her to initiate other priestesses who are opening to the mysteries of the divine feminine,

Next, there's the Edgewalker. The Edgewalker has a very unique quality of being connected to ancient wisdom while also being anchored in the future. She is a futurist and walks the edge of innovation and birthing of the new earth. However, she has a very different relationship with danger. She is here to initiate and be the initiated one.

When we combine them? The High Priestess-Edgewalker is the dangerous one... a fiercely loving woman who is dangerous to the status quo. That is the edge that she is walking.

Activation

Take a few deep breaths, allowing the breath to come in through the nose and moving out through the mouth with the sound of "ha." Taking just a few breaths to anchor into this moment, allowing the lower belly to soften more and more with each breath, releasing any holding in the solar plexus. Again, full breath breathing in through the nose, out through the mouth, feeling your seat, feeling the support of the ground underneath you.

Begin to feel the air on your hands, your skin, your face, noticing the temperature, slowly becoming aware that you are sitting on top of a very high mountain in a remote location. With your outer eyes closed in this reality, open your eyes on this mountain top. You look around to see no one—nothing. You have a rope to your right side. On the left, there's a bow and arrow. Just for a moment, you realize that you're feeling nervous, asking yourself, "What am I doing here? Do I know how to get out of here?"

As you look across the distance, you see that there's smoke under a Spire. It looks like there is chaos, and more and more, you feel that you don't want to be here and that you are somehow in the wrong place—because you actually don't know how to get out. When you look down, you have no idea how to repel down this mountain. You don't have the answer.

But then you look down, and you see the way that you're dressed. You're dressed for the part! So maybe, just maybe, there is a code inside you that does know exactly what to do in this moment. You turn around and see a small puddle of water on this mountaintop, so you go over and look into it. And as you're looking into this puddle of water, you do not like what you see. She is ugly. You realize you are not the pretty face you've been presenting to the world. You are dirty and messy. You say to yourself, "She looks like a dangerous woman."

Now, in this moment, as you stare into your own ugly reflection, the not-pretty reflection, you realize that there is a part of you that gets to die now so that you can embody yourself fully in this moment and get out of here alive. Otherwise, you're going to be stuck on this mountaintop. And so, as you continue to gaze into your reflection and this puddle of water on this mountain, the sound of the wind swirling, you allow the reflection to tell you what is the part of you that gets to die.

Listen.

Keep breathing into your belly as you listen, keeping your belly soft. And when you receive the part that gets to die, claim it for yourself. Maybe it's the people pleaser, the good girl, the smart girl... Maybe it's the appropriate mother, the appropriate wife, or the appropriate daughter. Maybe it's the respectable woman or the one who's been afraid her whole life.

Whatever it is for you, claim it for yourself. Then, feel your readiness to let this part of you die so that you can LIVE... rather than dying on this mountain top. Right?

Just as you realize that you are willing to do this, you hear a sound, and a big, beautiful, fantastical, and majestic bird comes and sits. It is as tall as you are. When you stand, you see that this huge and mystical bird has landed on your mountain top. And you know that when you grab your bow and arrow and your rope and you grab onto this bird, and you climb on its back, that will be the moment that the part that needs to die gets to die. And you get to claim your life as a dangerous woman, dangerous to everything ready to be destroyed. Everything that does not work, everything that is corrupt. You do not need to be accepted, liked, or approved of. You cannot be shamed. You do not care to wash your face. You do not care about losing weight, and you are not afraid.

You climb onto the bird's back, and together you fly towards the fire, feeling the wind in your hair. You are indeed a dangerous woman, High Priestess EdgeWalker.

Taking a deep breath into the belly, you take flight. And this bird is bringing that self back into this moment right here, right now.

Feel the support of your groundedness. Go ahead and give a squeeze to your thighs, your knees, your hands before you open your eyes. Remember what died. Remember that you cannot be shamed, and you have no need for approval. And yes, you are dangerous in the best possible way.

Journal and Integrate

In this powerful activation of the High Priestess EdgeWalker, which part of you died? Journal about it as you anchor it into your body.

Free Gift

THE SAFETY PRACTICE: A 20-MINUTE DAILY EMBODIMENT PRACTICE

This is an embodiment practice so you can stay in your body as you express yourself. This practice offers deep healing from traumas that have affected a sense of safety, or your own choices that may have affected the balance of the first energy center, whose primary function is to give you permission to belong.

Access here >> anahitajoon.pages.ontraport.net/opt-safety

Biography

ANAHITA JOON is a modern-day priestess, healer, medicine woman, and credentialed spiritual counselor. Born into Iran's Islamic Revolution, her work today is the culmination of over 25 years of intensive study with mystic masters and shamans, social research, and over a decade of her own teaching and facilitation. As a Feminine Leadership mentor, Anahita activates the sacred leadership of women, leaving no stone unturned in awakening and unleashing the force of nature every woman carries within.

Learn more at **anahitajoon.com.**

The Queen

by Kenlyn Kolleen

Every woman is born with the energy of the Queen already inside her. The Queen is the sovereign self of a woman. She is there from the beginning, and she will never go away, even if repressed and never taken out of the dark. For many women, the Queen appears later in life, as you will see below, but on rare occasions she can be seen in young girls, even if that energy is not yet mature or refined. For example, I'm thinking of a funny YouTube video that went viral. It was of a little girl dancing on stage with other young ballerinas. She must have noticed that her parents weren't looking at her. In her pink tutu, the camera shows her stopping her twirls and vigorously pointing to herself with a stern look as if to say, "Hey, eyes up here. I'm the show." It was hilarious. I remember being in awe of her boldness and applauding her clarity to demand what she wanted.

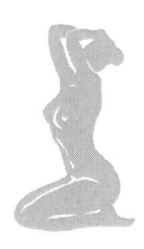

MY STORY

I wasn't one of those girls. I was shy and attention scared me. Over time I learned to use force to compensate for that fear. Some women do the opposite and become more people-pleasing or demure. Either way, both strategies are attempts to avoid the real power of the Queen.

It wasn't until a couple of years before I turned 50 that I began to seek advice from Wise Women (also called Crones) about aging. I could feel shifts taking place in my body and psyche that I wanted to understand. I needed a more powerful context for aging than the one society was about to hand me. So I consulted with two women who had written and taught about divine feminine archetypes. It was through them that I learned about the archetype of the Queen.

Sheila Foster, the founder of Temple of the Sacred Feminine, shared the four innate feminine archetypes who sit in a mandala and represent the directions—the Lover, Mother, Medial Woman, and Amazon Woman. In the center of the mandala is the Queen. Later, I quoted Sheila in my book, The Art of Turning 50, "The Queen knows who she is and accepts herself as she is." Radical Self-Acceptance. That's next-level Queen-ship.

The other Wise Woman who impacted me deeply was my former therapist, Jude Blitz—one of the wisest women in my life—who shared her view of the Queen based on the trajectory of a woman's life in chronological order: Maiden, Mother, Queen, and Wise Woman.

I was coming out of the Mother-phase of my life, although I wouldn't have named it that at the time since I didn't have children of my own, Yet now I see I was engaged in a lot of mothering: caring for animals, advocating for causes on behalf of the innocent, maintaining a household with step-children, and climbing the career ladder as a lawyer (yes, you can mother your career). Those mothering activities took passion, tireless energy, and personal sacrifice.

When I learned that the Queen was my next stage of life, my whole body tingled with aliveness. It felt congruent with the subtle changes taking place inside my being. I felt that something I had never before experienced was coming online. That tingling was my inner-knowing telling me, "The Queen is here!" The Queen has an entirely different frequency from the Mother, no matter if she's still in the midst of raising children, at the height of her career or starting over in life.

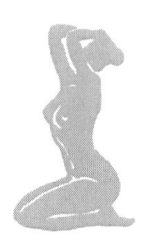

THE NATURE OF QUEEN ENERGY

Let's take a moment to understand Queen energy, as she is a particularly important archetype for women to activate in midlife.

At the core of the Queen is sovereignty. Sovereignty means "home rule." It doesn't mean ruling over other people. Rather, the Queen is the ruler of herself. In fact, all people are sovereign, but most don't know it. Most people are asleep to who they really are. To know yourself as sovereign is to know yourself as the responsible party in your life. Response-able. You're able to respond to life from a place of choice. It takes a lot of courage to assume the throne of your life. It's much easier to blame, pine, grasp, wish for, live for, fantasize, or sulk—even though it's ultimately more painful.

The awareness of responsibility is the power card in your life. Without it, you are a victim to life, circumstances, other people, the way you grew up, and what happened to you in past lives or your childhood.

Once you matter to yourself and treat yourself as if you matter to yourself, your world changes. No longer are you self-sacrificing, overreaching, people pleasing, or throwing away your precious life force energy. Life takes on greater clarity and ease, even if it takes applied will and commitment to build the new muscle of Queen-ship.

Sovereignty restores your choice. It restores your agency. Its central axiom is "I matter to myself."

Today, I'm well into my 50s and embodying my Queen, owning my sovereignty. Relishing in the world I create (whether I like it or not) is one of my main spiritual practices—and it IS a practice. I have grown in my personal power as I embody my Queen.

Without my inner Queen, I would never have had the courage or capacity to become an embodied feminine leader, facilitate powerful and connected global groups of women in the Divine Feminine Inner Circle, and train women to be leaders and make money sharing their gifts through my Divine Feminine Business Mastery program. The more I follow the truth that expresses itself through me, the easier life becomes. Life is a mirror. In that mirror, I see and get to experience myself as love, challenges, shadow, light, and grace. My growth is constant and relentless. I accept this because no matter what happens, I have myself. That is true gold.

WHY IS THE QUEEN IMPORTANT FOR THE NEW PARADIGM?

The Queen archetype is the foundation of the Divine Feminine RISING. Without the Queen activated in the feminine, the feminine would remain in a victim position vis-à-vis the patriarchy. It's easy to blame the wounded masculine and patriarchal system for perpetrating centuries of lies, abuse, and psychological war games on Mother Earth, who is the feminine herself, and on all beings including other men, women, children, and all species of plants, animals and sea life. For the feminine to take her rightful place in influencing, governing, leading, and co-creating the new paradigm, she must know who she is, accept herself as she is, know how truth feels in her body, be committed to follow that truth at all costs, turn away from not truth, use her voice, value her contribution, live as if she matters, and be responsible for all that she creates in her life, not as a form of blame but as a stand that she is the creator of her own life.

When the feminine restores her power to herself by activating her Queen, which she repeatedly does through practice and remembrance, she opens herself to receive the many archetypes and energies of the divine feminine who want to express themselves through her. The Queen is the portal into them all.

Activation

Read through the instructions of the activation before beginning.

If you're getting chills reading this, I suspect you're ready to assume the throne and crown yourself Queen of your life. It doesn't matter your age or stage in life; you will discover layers to your Queen as she reveals new aspects of herself with the crossing of the many thresholds in your life—welcoming and caring for a child, getting married or divorced, turning 50, experiencing the death of your parents or other loss, starting over, transitioning between major life events or awakening spiritually, to name a few.

BEGIN WITH GROUNDING + BREATH PRACTICE

BEGIN by standing up with your bare feet on the floor or directly on the Earth.

OPEN your palms so that they are facing forward in a receiving position.

CLOSE your eyes.

FEEL the frequency of Mother Nature through your feet. Draw in her energy through your feet, your legs, your womb, your solar plexus, your heart, your throat, your third eye, and up to your crown.

CIRCULATE that energy back down to your feet. Repeat a few times.

BREATHE long and deep as you draw the energy up and exhale fully and completely as you circulate the energy back down.

Repeat until you feel that you are fully in your body.

BEGIN THE QUEEN CHAKRA ACTIVATION PRACTICE

PLACE your attention on each area of your body and activate the Queen energy in each chakra. Feel free to touch each area with your hands and send healing and activation energy through your palms into that area of your energetic body.

ROOT – Activate the Queen of Abundance. Feel the abundance of Gaia herself coming up through your feet into your root. She has always held you. Her energy is resourceful, abundant, and regenerative. Affirmation: I am safe. I am cared for. I am Nature. I am abundant.

SACRAL – Activate the Queen of Creativity and Sensuality. Feel your womb space. Bring life energy to this space. Affirmation: My womb is a place of life, creation, and pleasure. My womb is a portal to the Mystery.

SOLAR PLEXUS – Activate the Queen of Confidence. Claim your confidence. No one can give it to you. You must give it to yourself. Affirmation: I know who I am. I accept who I am.

HEART – Activate the Queen of Compassion and Neutrality. The heart unifies the lower triangle of base instinctual energies with the upper triangle with angelic energies. The heart is equanimous and neutral. Place your hands in prayer pose with your thumbs touching your sternum. Generate compassion and a neutral mind by witnessing judgments without affirming them. Affirmation: My heart dissolves all polarity and rests in compassion.

THROAT – Activate the Queen of Your Voice. Open your throat chakra by using your voice. First, feel into your essential nature. Let it bubble up. Here's your moment to declare who you are to yourself out loud. Affirmation: Who I am is ____[add a potent word here like Love or Power or Joy]! Say it as many times to yourself in the mirror until you believe it. Dig deep and say it from your navel.

THIRD EYE – Activate the Queen of Your Intuition. Close your eyes and look at the brow point inside your head. Activate the glandular system. Become completely calm and slow your breath. Affirmation is in the form of a question to ask yourself: "What do I know?" Listen.

CROWN – Activate the Queen of Your Divinity. Close your eyes and roll them to look at the top of your head from the inside. Allow your crown to open to the Divine. You are a bridge between heaven and earth. Imagine a stream of light pouring into your crown from the Divine. Affirmation: I am the Light of My Soul. I am Divine.

ETHERS – Activation the Queen of Your Connection to the Multiverse. With your eyes closed, move your awareness outside of your body. Imagine it as shimmering gold light around your body in the shape of an egg. It's below you, above you, and all around you. Feel the quality of that light against your skin. Feel how expansive your vibration is, including and beyond your body.

TO END:

Take a few deep breaths. Slowly flutter open your eyes.

Play some good tunes and DANCE. Celebrate your Queen. For some musical suggestions, listen to my Divine Feminine Summit playlist on Spotify at: bit.ly/divinefemininesummit

Journal and Integrate

1. What are the ways that you demonstrate that you don't matter in your life? Who are you blaming for your life?

2. *What story would you have to confront about yourself if you believed that (and thus acted like) you mattered?*

– *The Queen* –

3. *How can you restore integrity to yourself by being responsible for your experiences? (Remember: responsible doesn't mean that it's your fault or that you caused the situation. Responsibility is not true or untrue. It's simply a way to restore integrity to yourself and access to your personal power.)*

4. Where do you feel your Queen in your body?

5. What is your Queen telling you about what's true for you right now?

6. *As you step into your Queen, what becomes possible for you?*
7. *What chakra in the exercise above needs more of your attention?*

– The Queen –

Free Gift

TOP TEN ACTIVATIONS OF THE DIVINE FEMININE SUMMITS 2020 AND 2021

The Divine Feminine lives in you. She is in each of us in the form of feminine energies. Those energies want to be expressed, especially now.

Join curator and host of the Divine Feminine Summit, Kenlyn Kolleen, in activating over 30 divine feminine energies so that you can align with your true purpose and increase your impact and income.

KENLYN's GIFT to you is the Top Ten activations of the Divine Feminine Summits 2020 and 2021. These ACTIVATIONS are part interview and part embodied awakening of that divine feminine energy in you through meditation, dance, or affirmation. Archetypes include Mystical Sage, Gaia, Wise Woman, Kali Ma, High Priestess Edgewalker, and more.

Access here >> kenlynkolleen.com/free-gift

Biography

KENLYN KOLLEEN is a premiere leadership, empowerment + spiritual business coach, and curator of The Divine Feminine Summit, a global sisterhood dedicated to empowering the voice of the feminine. Through private one-on-one coaching, empowerment circles + retreats, and warmly expansive online spaces, Kenlyn strives to be an accessible connective force for all.

Feeling the call to support women to reclaim their power—spiritually, emotionally, and financially—Kenlyn moved beyond her former life as a top-of-her-class Notre Dame law graduate and attorney to focus on empowering women to embody their radiance, live their purpose, and make a significant impact on behalf of our planet.

As her experiences taught her to embrace a higher law and seek higher truths, she moved away from the corporate world and toward India. Her first spiritual pilgrimage included a private audience with His Holiness the Dalai Lama. She returned from her second as a Kundalini Yoga teacher.

Kenlyn is the author of The Art of Turning 50: A Woman's Guide to a Radiant, Authentic Life, and teaches Kundalini RISING Yoga via her international livestream platform. As a filmmaker, her short film Doglama catalyzes others to explore spiritual lessons on loving and letting go. In addition, she has served on the board of Free A Child in Nepal and launched the first anti-trafficking program in Denver, Colorado, serving homeless and vulnerable youth.

Kenlyn lives, breathes, and connects in California, and a few other magical places around the world.

Visit KenlynKolleen.com or watch her film, Doglama, at: **kenlynkolleen.com/meet-kenlyn.**

Visit her on Facebook in her private groups at Divine Feminine Sisterhood RISING at **facebook.com/groups/584914838986655** and Kundalini RISING Yoga at **facebook.com/groups/607252239624737.**

Visit her on Instagram at **instagram.com/evolvingsisters/**

TAKE THE NEXT STEP

If you'd like to take the next step in working with your Queen, purchase a copy of *The Art of Turning 50* on Amazon or Kindle. The entire book is a workbook and a journal to get you deeper into your Queen and to create a ritual with your sisterhood to witness, acknowledge and celebrate this rite of passage. Even if you're not yet 50 or well past it, *The Art of Turning 50* is an excellent guide for transitions.

Listen to an excerpt of Chapter 1 here: **kenlynkolleen.com/the-art-of-turning-50**

Saraswati

by Jeanie Manchester

Many years ago, while practicing yoga, I became aware of the energy behind my breath. I sensed a subtle vibration in the rise and fall of each inhale and exhale. It was truly astonishing, as I knew that I was touching into the mystical energy at the heart of life. As the years passed, I have learned that my experience was ONE with the living pulse of consciousness: The Goddess Chit Shakti. Shakti means power and Chit means consciousness, which refers to the feminine principle or life force behind all things. This power fuels everything; the sun, moon, stars, flowers, trees, as well as our very own heartbeat. Our body, heart, mind, thoughts, and emotions are made of Shakti. Shakti makes up everything in the relative world. The Shakti is said to be like a wave in the ocean. The wave can look as if it's moving apart from the ocean, but it's never really separate. This is our struggle as humans—we are like the wave. We think we are separate from the ocean and, therefore, separate from consciousness. The truth is, we are made of consciousness, so we are never truly severed or split from Shakti. This unity within diversity is at the heart of human suffering and awakening.

Many of us have had experiences like I did in yoga. You wake up to the beauty and expansion in life, only to forget it in stressful moments when doubt and insecurity arise.

This happened one day when my beloved teacher spontaneously popped into my class. "What do I know?" I whispered to myself. Even worse, "What if I say something wrong?" A feeling of doubt overtook me. I turned red and my throat became so parched I could hardly swallow. Just a few minutes after his arrival, I could hardly speak. I remember falling into what felt like a defining sea of self-deprecation. In these moments, it's like everything I studied and cared about for so many years vanished in an instant.

The Tantric tradition says we play a game (Lila) of Hide & Go Seek with the divine. We remember and forget our true creative power. In an instant, we cling to our doubt and fear rather than trust our inner guide and our outer capacities. We all have had moments where insecurity and doubt overtake us and we have challenges to overcome. Did you know that Amanda Gorman, the youngest inaugural poet and award-winning writer, grew up with a speech impediment? She is a great example of overcoming physical and emotional challenges. Amanda not only overcame a speech impediment but has stepped into new creative heights.

Amanda's capacities as an artist of speech are best represented in the goddess archetype of Saraswati. Saraswati is not only the goddess of speech but also of the creative arts, computer sciences, music, poetry, writing, and teaching. On Inauguration Day, January 2021, Amanda Gorman stepped fully into her Saraswati shoes as she delivered "The Hill We Climb," an elegant and powerful recitation of her poetry. Listening to Amanda, it was difficult to imagine that she struggled with her speech at all. Her poetry was crystal clear, inspiring, powerful, and elegant. She overcame a huge speech blockage that took courage, commitment, and a lot of inner work. She also had to "practice" becoming the poet she is today by falling and getting back up.

Like Amanda, I had to overcome my fear and trust my inner gauge. This takes commitment, courage, patience, and hours of practice. Each day, I go to my love of teaching, to the art of articulation, speech, and the joy of sharing this with others. When my inner critic rears her ugly head, I turn to mantra, singing, playing harmonium, and laughter as a balm for my soul. Meditation is a powerful tool to shift our negativity and is a part of my daily "shakti tune-up."

Saraswati consciousness teaches us to trust in our intuitive capacities, harness our gifts and creative talents, and endeavor something great with life. She also shows us where we hide out: where we have fallen asleep and where our energies for creative expression are limited. As Marianne Williamson says, "Who are you to play small?" The Great Goddess of consciousness, the energy behind your life is actively calling you forth to heal and to make something outrageous with your life.

If we are to change our negative thoughts and inhibiting beliefs, we must attend to the subtle body where our memories are held. One of the ways to enter into a more intimate relationship with Goddess Saraswati is through mantra. Mantra broken down means" Manas" or mind and "tra" to traverse. Mantras are vibratory tools that move across subtle bands inside us to release negative memories, patterns, and beliefs that plague our lives. While the most potent mantra technology is given under proper guidance in a special ceremony called "puja," which activates a given mantra, we can start with a more general understanding of mantra usage here.

Sarawati's bija or seed mantra is "A I M." When we repeat her mantra, it has an impact on our subtle body. Repeating her mantra daily can bring about a feeling of well-being and joy and helps to move energy in the area of the throat. I find her mantra powerful before I teach, write, or give a speech.

When we align with the sacred every day, we free up our contracted energy. This is key for healing our wounds and rising into our creative potential. Our devotion to the sacred surely moves our personal lives positively forward. Yet, this devotion is never just about our solo journey. We are here on planet Earth to collectively heal, to help each other rise into a new paradigm of living more peacefully, consciously harnessed to the divine. As more and more people awaken to the living life force we call Shakti, the more we contribute to global healing and make a bigger impact on the future healing of our precious planet Earth.

To all of you who question your abilities and are afraid to stand in who you are, you must call on Goddess Durga. She is Queenly, filled with regal radiance, fierce, and merciless. She is the one that will carry you beyond your wildest inhibitions and greet you at the gate of peace, liberation, and love to say, "Job well done."

Activation

Take a comfortable seat. Take a moment to feel deeply into the vibration that is within you. Feel your sit bones sink into your chair.

Begin to consider the last several days of your life and any misunderstandings you've had with others and yourself around something that you said, or a gesture that felt misaligned. Maybe you were jealous? Saraswati in her shadow form can feel jealous of her sisters—And yet when we are fully in our autonomy, we don't need that kind of recognition. We already feel complete and whole.

On your inhale, breathe in the pearly luminous light of Saraswati and recite the following mantra ten times:

OM AIM SARASWATYAI NAMAH

Close your eyes. Deepen your breath.

Allow the mantra to move into your internal awareness. Inhale Saraswati's luminous pearl light. As you exhale, allow that white pearly light to move through your body and mind into your toes and into the earth.

Inhale again. Infuse the body with pearly white light. And as you exhale, allow the light to move through your body, releasing any fear, feelings of doubt, shame, or inadequacy. They all go out with the exhale. Keep infusing the body with the pearly white light with your inhale.

As you continue to breathe with the pearly light, sit with the following questions: What am I here to express in this life? How are my gifts and talents moving through me as my creative power?

Allow the answers to flow toward you as effortlessly as water flows.

You can sit in the silence as long as you need.

When you feel complete, begin to softly open your eyes. Pick up your journal and pen and record what came to you. Try to write with no judgment or filter.

Journal and Integrate

1. Practice Saraswati Mantra Jej
   Take a comfortable seat, close your eyes, and bring a situation in your life that needs clarity and direction. Write it down in your journal. Now chant her mantra 11 times ("OM AIM SARASWATEYE NAMAHA"). Sit in silence for 2 minutes and then drop your question into the silence. Wait, listen, and receive any insight that bubbles up inside you. Avoid trying to make an answer come from your mind. Journal spontaneously about what is arising. For potency, repeat daily for a full lunar cycle.

2. *"Stretch your Wings"*
   Challenge yourself to an art, speaking, computer, musical instrument, or singing/chanting or cooking class.

3. *"Stand on the Ledge of Freedom"*
   Freedom arises when we stop identifying with old, negative memories. Practice 20 minutes of daily meditation.

4. *"Turn your Kleshas into Lakshmi's"*
    In the Tantric tradition, we say: Practice turning a negative situation into a positive, upflifting experience.

– *Divine Feminine Aligned Journal* –

Free Gift

POWER OF THE SPOKEN WORD

The Power of the Spoken Word: A Guided Saraswati Devi Meditation
Access here >> **jeaniemanchester.com/free-meditation**

Biography

JEANIE MANCHESTER is the founder of Anjaneya Yoga Shala in Boulder, CO. She is a Master Yoga Teacher and Meditation Instructor with over 30 years of dedicated practice. Her signature classes are rooted in bhakti chant, storytelling, mantra, mudra, and meditation. As a senior student and Acharya of Neelakantha Meditation, she initiates people into this elegant and potent mantra practice. She is also an avid student of the Sri Vidya Goddess tradition of South India.

Jeanie's path of the divine feminine and awakening of kundalini Shakti has given rise to new inspiration in her life and all of those she trains. Her students love her heart-based, friendly style of intuitive mentoring and teaching. She is the creator and guide of the Shakti Sisterhood as well Goddess Guidance monthly membership and the Founder of The Planetary Awakening Summit. These offerings are dedicated to "Women on the Rise!" She supports the householder woman's spiritual journey both by embracing her shadow and pain and moving towards an empowered way of living life. Jeanie offers teacher training, meditation guidance, spiritual and business mentoring, and leads retreats and immersions to wondrous places around the globe.

When not on her mat or cushion, Jeanie is found hiking or skiing in the beautiful Colorado wilderness that is dear to her heart. She lives in Boulder, CO, with her husband, two adult children, and dog, Rosie.

Phoenix Rising

by Catherine Grace O'Connell

Every woman has a Goddess inside of her. Some women recognize this and meld with the Goddess over time and become one. Some women never find belief in their own Self and power, and the Goddess does not truly manifest. Occasionally, the Goddess herself senses a purpose and a need for her presence and will remain subdued no longer. The result is not subtle.

The Goddess calls upon and becomes the Phoenix.

The Phoenix can rise within each and every one of us at different times and for different reasons. The Phoenix rose at a pivotal time in my life, following a Near Death Experience. Trauma and illness had broken me, and I had no desire to continue living. Like so many women, I spent much of my life living for others, suppressing and repressing my Authentic Self and soul's desires. Our soul and our true Self cannot remain silenced and suppressed forever. It takes immense energy to hold your true Self back, to stop her from rising. I discovered that once the Phoenix was ready, the force for her to rise was so great that I was powerless to hold her back. Much of me burned away in white-hot flames. What remained was beautiful and powerful... and eager to find her purpose!

The power of the Phoenix is that, in an instant, the false Self burns away, leaving behind the essence of who you truly are. What falls away are the ashes, those aspects of us that were never real. They were temporary, borrowed for a while, but no longer needed. For me, the rise of the Phoenix meant meeting and greeting a beautiful new life along with an entirely new Self: my Goddess Self. There's a freedom, a lightness of being, that takes place once the Phoenix has paid a visit. This Goddess is a fierce force, one full of power and grace. Her authentic power is here to point a woman in the direction of her true north, her soul's true purpose. She's also there to help us to get out of our own way. Often, the greatest obstacles in life are the ones we've created for ourselves. We've unconsciously plopped them down right in front of us, blocking all the good the Universe has awaiting us. Then we wonder why the hell they showed up. We hold ourselves back, much of the time believing we're unworthy, only to crush our Spirit and our Divine Essence. The Phoenix is there to serve us, to help us break free from the chains and bonds we have unnecessarily placed upon ourselves.

I believe within every woman lies an alter ego, a true Self she has yet to meet, brimming with power, personality, and limitless possibility. Her Authentic Self is often buried deep beneath layers of pain, trauma, wounds, and most of all, old stories, beliefs, thoughts, mis-perceptions, judgments, patterns, and behaviors that no longer serve our soul.

The false self is no match for the power of the Phoenix. If the Goddess rises as the Phoenix, she will not be denied. The false self cannot withstand the light, power, beauty, and grace found in the Authentic Self—the Self that is indeed, the Goddess.

The Authentic Self is a force of its own. Authenticity is fuel. It's the catalyst, like a match to the Phoenix, giving her permission to rise and to allow the false self to burn away into the ashes. The false self keeps us small, squished, and squeezed, confining a soul that was never meant to be confined.

What is authenticity? It is freedom. Freedom from the inside. Freedom to love the heck out of ourselves and to turn our perceived flaws into strengths. Always remember that within the shadow lies the gold. The shadow blocks the light. A shadow cannot exist without light. On the other side of darkness is always light. When we shine a light in the darkness, the darkness recedes. Darkness cannot hold up to the power of light. Light is active and a place to shine. Darkness is passive and a place to hide. Our false self represents darkness. Our True Self represents light. We will never rise as far or as high as we will once we have come face to face with our Authentic Self, shedding dis-empowering stories and beliefs and stepping into the truth of who we are. That is when we become one with and embrace the Goddess.

2020 brought many of us to our knees. It stopped us in our tracks. Collectively, it forced us off a global proverbial treadmill—a treadmill that kept us from being present. When we are forced to our knees, we're given a wake-up call. In many ways, this was a gift—a gift of space, time for reflection. A global pause providing humanity with wide-open space—exactly what was required to do some deeply needed soul searching.

2020 was a gift to humanity. 2020 was an opportunity for global vibrational elevation. A Global Reset. 2021, the NOW is your reward.

The Phoenix is about rising from the ashes of our challenges. It is the ultimate transformational force to assist us in becoming the whole, complete, spiritual being we were born to be. The ashes are the parts of us we no longer need—those aspects no longer serving us, holding us back from our greater purpose here on earth—the ones beckoning to fall away, to alchemize into dust, while the truth of who we are is ready to rise. For many of us, Midlife is a time when the Phoenix makes her appearance. The life of a woman before the Midlife pivot usually comes loaded with lots of excess baggage—all kinds of things that aren't needed and aren't particularly helpful to propel a woman to a higher destination, to her soul's higher purpose.

We are in a new paradigm, a new Earth as Eckhart Tolle shares, one that exists at a higher vibration: one requiring us to elevate our personal vibration. 2020 was a Divine part of the plan, collectively, shaking loose many of our old ways of being all at once. The old ways of being and doing no longer work. The Phoenix doesn't mess around. She is pure energy that shows no mercy for those aspects of us no longer aligned with our Divine Self. That is the gift of the Phoenix. She's here for a purpose. She has work to do. When she's done, what remains is the purest essence of who we truly are—the higher vibrational aspects that allow us to live in a higher vibrational state to complete the work our souls came here to do. What remains is our Divine unshackled Soul filled with pure potentiality and limitless possibility.

The Phoenix shows up when we need her most. She doesn't tell you who you should be. She clears the path for you to be the woman you have always wanted to be!

She's the alter ego who exists within our heart and my soul. She is the best part of you, of me, of us. She's the woman we have always desired to be. She is the encapsulation of our hopes, our dreams, and our highest aspirations. She's the real you actualizing and alchemizing before your very eyes. Sure, there are days when we will deny her, days when we will repress her, days we don't allow her to be, constraining her from rising higher and higher, days the old stories begin to replay, days the old beliefs begin to take hold. And, then, we realize: That's not me. That's an old voice, an old self, our shadow, our inner child screaming for attention. At times, we let her scream. We give her space for a tantrum or two. We let her be. At least for a while. And, then we hold her. We comfort her. We encourage her.

I believe every woman has an alter ego, aspects of herself she's denied, suppressed or repressed. I also believe the answer to finding her lies within the pain, the wounds, the stories and most of all, the dreams and the desires. Be open, Dear One. Be open to diving deep… in the darkest and deepest depths of your being. Within the dark crevasse lies the gold, the jewel, the possibility, and the dream. Pay attention to those dreams, to your heart's deepest desires. They exist for a reason.

We find ourselves in a new paradigm, one where the Divine Feminine is now in charge. The Goddess Energy that's been held back since the beginning of Creation, has been unleashed. To reach the highest heights in this new energy requires us to lighten our load, to let go of anything that keeps us small, confining the beauty and power of the human spirit. Accepting this gives you the power. What that means is that it's time to invite the Phoenix to join you in releasing aspects of you no longer serving you, those egoic parts of yourself—thoughts, beliefs, attitudes, patterns, and behaviors—that aren't serving your highest good. Think of the Phoenix as your best friend, the ultimate Badass. The fire she brings is Fierce. The Phoenix knows what stays and what goes. She's deliberate and discerning. Invite her into your heart and your soul. Join with her to ascend into the new energy with a lightness of being and a soul full of purpose and passion. Watch the Phoenix Rise from the ashes, the Phoenix that is you, the truth of who you are, so you can be all that you can be.

Activation

This exercise is a Heart Activation to assist in letting go of aspects of ourselves that no longer serve us.

Begin by closing your eyes. Take a few deep, centering breaths. Breathe in for a count of four. Hold for a count of four. Breathe out for a count of four. Allow your body to relax. Now, picture in your mind's eye, your head (your mind) gently floating off of your shoulders, up into the ether. Allow your mind to softly float away. Pause and take two deep, centering, grounding breaths.

Keeping your eyes closed, take your attention and begin dropping it down into your heart. Place your hand on your heart and allow your inner eye, your focus to be on your heart. Take three deep breaths in and out of your heart.

Now, you are in your heart's center, the purest part of you—who you truly are.

Take a moment and picture a loved one or something that you love. It could be a child, a parent, a friend. It can also be an animal, a puppy, a kitten, or even a beautiful setting in nature. Anything that brings you into a state of peace and love.

Place that image right into your heart's center. Now, take three slow, deep, centering breaths in and out of your heart. Allow your awareness and your consciousness to fully drop into your heart. (This will activate and radiate your heart's energy, our largest energy field.)

Now that you are in a space of love and deeply connected to your Divine Self, ask yourself the question, "Who Am I?" Ask this question to yourself three times. Pause, and wait for an answer to arise from deep within. The answer emanates from your Soul and not your mind.

Now, take three more deep breaths, breathing in for a count of four, holding for a count of four, and letting your breath out for a count of four.

Pause.

Ask yourself, "What am I ready to let go of?" Ask yourself this question slowly three times and wait for the answer to arise from within.

When you have your answer, take a moment to thank those aspects of yourself for helping you. Now, invite the Phoenix in to partner with you. Ask her to help you let go of those parts of you no longer needed. Allow her Divine Presence to hold you while you place these aspects into a bubble of light and send them up into the light and allow them to dissolve. Invite the energy of the Phoenix to transform these aspects into ashes and allow them to fall away. Thank this beautiful Goddess for helping you in your transformation.

Now, that you have created space inside of you by letting go of aspects of you that are no longer serving you, fill that space consciously and intentionally with something positive. It can be something you wish to bring into your life. It can be a quality you wish to activate inside of you. It can be anything that comes from your heart and lights up your spirit.

Now, take three more deep breaths—breathe in for a count of four, hold for a count of four, and breathe out for a count of four.

When you are ready, open your eyes and greet your new Self with love.

Journal and Integrate

What is my soul's true purpose and what can I let go of to fully align with the highest part of my being?

In what way have I been holding myself back from the good the Universe is trying to send my way?

Am I ready to invite the Phoenix into my being to help me to break those chains and set my soul free?

- Phoenix Rising -

Free Gift

MASTERING MODERN MIDLIFE—FREE E-BOOK

7 Powerful Tips for Finding Your Confidence at Midlife

Access here >> catherinegraceo.com/start-mastering-modern-midlife-today

Biography

CATHERINE GRACE O'CONNELL is an Ageism Positivist, an Empowerment Catalyst, the Founder of The Forever Fierce Revolution, a global Facebook Community dedicated to supporting and celebrating the Modern Midlife Woman, and the CEO of MODLife Media, a female-focused message-based digital media agency.

Learn more at **catherinegraceo.com**.

Black Jaguar Medicine Woman

A RITUAL

By Tanya Lynn

In October 2020, my husband Brent and I felt the call to pack up all our belongings, two kids and cat to move down to Costa Rica.

This adventure into the wild jungle has been and continues to be guided by a power higher than ourselves. We have been following the nudges from the universe. A big part of this is an initiation to claim my medicine woman.

A symbolic animal of this initiation is the black Jaguar.

The intention of this ritual is to gain clarity on your power and trust in the mystery of the wild feminine. The symbolic meaning of the black jaguar is

"Unfamiliar Territory, Grace, Darkness." When you find yourself in unfamiliar territory, the jaguar walks with you into the unknown future with grace and trust. She reminds you to look for the light instead of focusing on the dark.

You may not have all the answers right now, and that's okay. Embrace it. Trust that life will reveal the answers step by step.

Look closely at the jaguar, who is also a panther. She has a condition called melanism. When you examine closely, the typical markings on her black coat tell who she really is.

Who are you, up close and personal?

Activation

What do you want to gain clarity on in your life right now?

What fears have you been experiencing?

What unresolved traumas have been coming up for you?

VISUALIZATION

Close your eyes, taking some deep breaths in, relaxing your body.

Bring your attention into your heart and just feel whatever is in your heart right now. Maybe you're excited. Maybe you've had some anxiety. Whatever it is that you've been experiencing in your heart, just take a moment to acknowledge it.

Relax your jaw, your shoulders, and your hips. Come into your body.

Now imagine that you are in the jungle. See yourself on the bottom floor of the jungle with all these huge trees with vines coming down. It's vibrant green and lush. Feel the vibrancy, the aliveness of all the plants. Feel the connection with nature in this green lush, tropical rainforest.

You can feel the moisture of the humidity, it's hot, and you feel yourself sweating a little bit.

You can hear the loud sound of the jungle, the insects, and birds. You see a blue butterfly flutter by.

You watch as a line of leaf cutter ants march with green leaves on their backs down a trail.

You follow them. Start to walk down this path in the jungle.

You hear rushing water, a river to your right.

You continue to walk, watching your step for rocks and other things that could make you trip, walking carefully through.

Feel the awe-inspiring, wild feminine nature of this jungle. Feel the mysterious, unknown, almost a little dangerous nature of this jungle.

Take some deep breaths, and repeat to yourself: "I'm safe here."

You come across a clearing. You approach this beautiful waterfall. It's coming down into a crystalline pool.

You sit down and put your feet in the water. Sitting there, gazing up at the trees, listening to the sounds.

You hear something behind you, so you turn your head, and there you see walking very slowly toward you, a beautiful black jaguar.

She's sauntering toward you, her sleek muscles glistening in the light.

She's such a big, powerful animal.

Here she comes, walking toward you. You feel alive and invigorated by her presence because she's so powerful.

She comes up to the pond and right next to you, she leans down to take a drink as you watch her. She's not concerned with you.

You watch the muscles as she moves. The way she slinks. The way she laps up the water with her giant tongue.

You are frozen, mesmerized by her sheer power.

She looks up with you. And she makes eye contact with you.

She has a message for you.

What's the medicine? What's the message?

As quickly as you make eye contact, she darts back into the jungle and is gone.

Feel your heart beating with the connection you had with her, the primal wild exquisite beast from the jungle, and what she brought up within you.

You get up and take that with you down the path, back through the jungle where you started.

Take a deep breath in and give gratitude...

Gratitude for the plants

Gratitude for the animals

Gratitude for the wild jungle

Gratitude for the medicine.

RELEASE

As we are on the conscious path of evolution, past life traumas come up to be healed.

These old traumas create low self-worth and a plethora of limiting beliefs such as:

the belief to work harder

the doubt that you don't deserve the goodness, you must suffer

the fear that you can't trust

the need for control

There is a war between your left and right brain trying to find sacred marriage within (masculine and feminine). That you must fight for your survival, that you must take because resources are limited, that you must dominate in order to be seen and heard.

Write down all the limiting beliefs that keep you at war with yourself, that have you fighting for control.

Burn this paper in the fire and let it go.

RECLAIM DANCE

Now it is time to step into your power as the black jaguar medicine woman.

Put on your sexy black dress.

Stand in front of the mirror and say to yourself:

"I am the source of my own power.

I let go of figuring it all out.

I give it up to the divine feminine to guide me through the mystery.

I trust in the divine flow."

Put on this song and dance to feel your source of power within:

Gajumaru—Yaima (yaimamusic.com): open.spotify.com/track/7cooh1IEHC8fXqsiCF25lF?si=6TgBKVvlT3Kg-Oh-L5B1klA

Lyrics:

[Verse 1]

Creating concrete visions of a macrocosmic prism with a brilliant optimism and appropriate ambition

To be open from the center redirected to the moment

This is it love, this is it love, unrestrainable nature

We can change it from the edges, we can challenge all our borders

There is always a new leader, there is always a new order

Our pathway is proceeding and the way is always changing

We are free from what prevents us to realise our destination

(ohhh, ohhh woho, ohhh, ohhh woho)

[Refrain]

Free, from all old stories I've been told, I walk through the valley of my own shadow

Free, from all old stories I've been told, I walk through the valley of my own shadow

[Verse 2]

Awareness is my virtue and I'm grateful for the search to

Dive deep within my own mind and to trust the intuition of the lives I've lived before this are essential form of gnosis it's a simple form of freedom it's as smooth as inhalation, oh the exhale is releasing all the tension I've been feeling, on the surface and beneath me I'm connecting to my spirit, and I'm here now right before you, I am present in this moment, my life's work is to honour the great beauty all around you

(ohhh, ohhh woho, ohhh, ohhh woho)

CLOSING

Give a prayer of gratitude to the black jaguar medicine woman. Place an image or symbol of her on your altar. Continue to visit her for 28 days.

Journal and Integrate

What message did black jaguar bring to you during this activation? What does it mean to you?

What limiting beliefs did you release in the fire ritual? How did it feel?

How did the dance affect your awareness of black jaguar medicine woman?

How are you embracing your power in a new way?

Free Gift

THE ART OF LEADING CIRCLE STARTUP KIT

Any woman can lead circle... you simply need a blueprint and a desire for connection. When women come together in sacred circle, magic happens. The power of women gathering is immeasurable: from healing the disconnection with the feminine to birthing new dreams and visions.

More and more women are seeking intentional circles for support, healing, transformation, and celebration. This startup kit offers women an opportunity to step into leadership and follow a step by step guide to create, lead and grow circles in their local community or online.

Access here >> sistershipcircle.com/sp/art-of-leading-circle-startup-kit/

Biography

TANYA LYNN is a "strategic activator" and the visionary CEO of Sistership Circle, a global organization that offers leadership training for women to reveal themselves and step into their power so they start their own circle business. Tanya has been internationally facilitating, coaching, and leading groups of women since 2006. Along her journey, she has found that balancing the masculine and feminine holds the secret to BEING a brave woman who is fully seen, heard, and celebrated as her true self while actualizing her dreams.

The Lover

by Ashley Fuller Rubin

Love is the most powerful force in the entire Cosmos.

So many of us women have neglected the archetype of "The Lover"—not necessarily consciously, but simply because we have been focused on our careers, or making ends meet, or focusing on making sure everyone's needs are met, except our own. Inside of these ways of being, we can become exhausted, depleted, and feel malnourished. We've been warriors in the world, standing for people and causes we believe in deeply, on a mission! But what's true is that without being a warrior who is ultimately standing for LOVE, we are missing out on the most powerful source (and force!) for change there is.

The lover is a flourishing archetype. She is in full Bloom. She is lush, juicy, and in the moment. She nourishes us deeply with her presence.

The lover is just that—she is a lover—a lover of life—a lover of others—a lover of the moment—a lover of beauty, and she also loves herself. She's creative and expressive in the most magnetic of ways.

She has a deep sense of relatedness and connection with all of life—and loves to love and care for those she loves, not in a mothering way—her way is as the lover.

The Lover is all about eros, sensuality, sexuality, creativity, relationships. I think of the lover as a lover of all of life in the manifest world. She is JUICY and Flourishing.

The Lover is so important, and she has been a deeply misunderstood archetype. She has been polarized at times as the virgin / whore, so many women have repressed this aspect in themselves, but we want to bring her BACK! And there's no better time than NOW, when we are empowered, and we're actually in the midst of creating a culture where it's safe for women to be fully expressed. We're certainly not there yet! But we're getting there. And part of our job as leaders is to create the way, to pave the way for women to be fully expressed in our world.

The Lover archetype has been in the background for many of us. When a woman has expressed it, it's often been misunderstood. But, alas the Divine Feminine is rising, we are reclaiming this energy inside of us. We are coming back into alignment with our nature.

Part of reclaiming The Lover in ourselves is coming back into our bodies and expressing ourselves through our bodies. Doing Yoga or dancing are such beautiful ways of bringing this into form—and, also, being in relationships where we aren't trying to fit into a mold of what we think that needs to look like. Relationships where we are fully expressed in our beingness—where there is a natural fluidity and flow between beings.

I have always been a very relational being. My relationships with others have been my greatest priority. As an example, I have friends in my life dating back to early childhood. Cultivating relationships has been a huge priority for me. I give great attention to this; as a result, I am very happy and fulfilled by my relationships with my husband, my daughters, my extended family, friends, and community. Even my pets! I can see how "The Mother" archetype has played out in my life, too, but clearly the dominant pattern has been that of "The Lover." It was no surprise to me when I took the quiz in the book (which I highly recommend!) The Goddess Within and scored highest with "Aphrodite."

And the influence of "The Lover" archetype goes back as far as I can remember! My parents have an old film clip of me from when I was about two-years-old where my father is holding me as I am leaning out toward my uncles trying to kiss their cheeks—unprovoked! I remember being fascinated by men from a very young age and wanting to play with boys.

I was given the "honor" of being voted "Biggest Flirt" in high school, where I had numerous boyfriends—here I was also expressing the shadow aspects of the archetype, being clearly more in love with the idea of love than with the boys who I was dating. Like Anna in the Disney film "Frozen," I was a hopeless romantic in those days, and was deeply confused and hurt by my experiences in love relationships then, sometimes because I was giving off an energy that was confusing for boys. I have always been quite sensual, enjoying the pleasures of life, including physical affection, and sometimes this just went too far for what I was actually comfortable with at the time. The boys were just as confused as I was (Hello, Aphrodite?!)

Sadly, though, my mother couldn't stand the expression of The Lover in me. She shamed me for it on several occasions (as many mothers and other women sadly will do if they haven't worked through their own shadows and wounds), as did many of the girls at school. I felt terribly misunderstood; this beautiful life force energy that I felt inside and was expressing was severely frowned upon by so many. It's vital for us, as we are reclaiming all parts of ourselves, to not shame ourselves or other women for this very natural, life-giving, life-affirming archetype if we are to truly, fully become our beautiful, Divine selves. In fact, it's vital for us to CELEBRATE her!

Love and loving have taken up much of my attention throughout my life, so much so that now I am known in my transformational coaching work as a "Love Evocateur!" Women share that they experience the transmission of love when they work with me. My coaching work over the past decade has been about not only supporting the awakening and activating of the feminine, it has also been about supporting the awakening and activating of the archetype "The Lover!"

Embracing all aspects of The Lover is part of this. In my work I am inspired to support women to move into their playful selves, and to live from their hearts; letting love lead. I mostly work with women who are rising into leadership roles; with me they are discovering how to open up to love, and letting love lead.

In my spiritual life, I love to love God / Spirit / The Divine—whatever name you give it. I feel my reciprocal, loving relationship with God deeply, and it is surely a love relationship I have cultivated! I think this is why Rumi's poetry appeals to me, as he speaks this love language with God so beautifully—better than anyone, in my opinion!

Another aspect of the lover archetype that I can see at play in my life is how I embrace beauty and creativity. I've enjoyed being a dancer, singer, and actress for decades and feel incredibly alive and expressed in these creative activities. When I'm in the audience, I easily weep witnessing the beautiful artistry of dancers, musicians, singers, performers, artists, etc... I also surround myself with beauty, and live with the intention of bringing beauty and love wherever I am, and wherever I go. My friends say I wear my heart on my sleeve, and that one of my best qualities is how I express my deep appreciation for them, and for all of life.

It is in all the ways I have illustrated that I can see how The Lover archetype has beautifully, profoundly impacted and influenced my life.

My wish is for you to open yourselves to the rich, juicy gifts "The Lover" will bring you.

Activation

A guided meditation to open your heart to love.

I invite you to close your nice deep breath… Just taking in some nice deep nourishing breaths—as if you could breathe all the way down into your hips… down into your low belly… Letting everything soften and widen here.

Imagine the breath is nourishing every cell in your body… and taking a scan of your body and just notice if there's anywhere where you're holding tension where tension doesn't actually need to be right now. And if you find that kind of tension anywhere, take a deep breath in and while you do that tighten up that spot as tight as you can, and on the exhale, let it go… and breathe as if you could breathe all the way down your legs, out the soles of your feet, and into the Earth... and contemplate the Earth for a moment; beautiful mother Earth.

And connecting to this beautiful source of flourishing life... This planet we are all part of... Feeling her...

And if you're sitting right now, take a moment to lean back in your chair. Move into a place of deep listening and receptivity...

And now, feel the energy of your heart.

If you'd like, you can place one or both of your hands on your heart.

Just getting deeply connected to your beautiful heart energy, and as you're leaning back, imagine energy is flowing TO you...

And start to notice the air on your skin—what does that feel like? Does it feel cool or warm? Is it dry or wet?

And whatever you're sitting or lying on, feeling where that meets your body. What does it feel like?

And noticing the sounds that you're hearing... they might be incredibly subtle... just noticing...

And noticing the aromas, as you take in a luxurious inhale, do you notice any scents?

And as you're doing this, tune into all of these sensual, sensuous expressions that are happening that you're able to receive and sense with your body.

And now moving into a place of gratitude and appreciation for your body and for all that you're able to feel and sense with it

See if you can find joy and pleasure in what you're sensing... whether it's the way something appears to your eyes... all the colors you can take in, lines, curves, shapes... or how something sounds... a gentle whisper, a voice... A song... all the pleasurable aromas you get to smell, imagine a gorgeous flower in bloom... imagine leaning in and taking in her incredible scent... and the tastes you get to taste... imagine a succulent, juicy piece of fruit and savoring that—the taste of this fruit, taking your time... and imagine the textures you get to feel with your hands and fingers... and the way things feel on your skin...

Feel into your heart, the energy here, the energy of love... and Invite your heart to open, and this energy of love to expand and grow... And imagine the energy of love just emanating outward from you... imagine loved ones, friends, pets, those beloveds in your life who are so dear to you, and extending your love to them right from your open heart, and then imagine them giving love back to you now, and just receive it! Allow it to flow into your heart, filling your whole being...

I encourage you now to move out into your day, into your world with your heart open—open to extend love to people out in the world, and to take in and receive all the beauty and pleasures of our world.

And if you can, I encourage you now to put on your favorite love song or a song that makes you happy... And DANCE!!!!

Journal and Integrate

I most deeply desire to experience and express in love...
I deeply desire a lover who...

The Lover

I love...
I feel most loved when...

I feel beautiful when...
I take pleasure in...

– *The Lover* –

What I love most about myself is...

Free Gift

ACTIVATING "THE LOVER" ARCHETYPE MEDITATION

A relaxing, guided meditation set to music, just for you: Evoking the Feminine Archetype of Beauty, Love & Creativity: "The Lover"

Access here >> ashleyfullerrubin.com/thelovermeditation

Biography

ASHLEY FULLER RUBIN has been a senior certified Feminine Power transformational coach, facilitator, and leader for over ten years. She's also the Community Director for the world-renowned Feminine Power Art of Love programs. Ashley has worked with thousands of women through private coaching and in facilitating women's "Power Circles," supporting each woman to have breakthroughs and leap into her vision for extraordinary life and love.

Ashley is a "Love Evocateur," deeply committed to empowering women to awaken and embrace the Feminine; attract and/or deepen and evolve love; embrace the art and science of dating (and have fun with it!); develop radical self-love and acceptance, and nourishing self-care; and activate feminine radiance to let their unique, radiant light shine BRIGHT, and fully become the women they came here to be—all in the spirit of "You really CAN (and deserve to!) have it all!"

Learn more at **ashleyfullerrubin.com**.

Divine Mother Narayani

by Brahmankyrie Shanti

Om Namo Narayani

Divine Mother Narayani has been the guiding force in my life, even when I wasn't aware of Her. I had no relationship with Her or any other divine power in my younger years and spent most of my time trying to escape my life. I spent my earlier years heavily addicted to drugs, alcohol, and crime from the age of 10 to 27. In the end, crack cocaine was my master—I had a bad habit of staying in abusive and dangerous relationships. You see, I was very comfortable in chaos and could not break free from the elusive pull of the darkness. The karmic debt of this lifetime was heavy-handed, to say the least. I struggled for many years until I finally surrendered and crawled into recovery a month shy of my twenty-eighth birthday.

This is the age of Kaliyuga, the age of sin. It is very easy in an era such as this one to be dragged down by all the darkness and low vibration. People struggle to remember their inherent worth and, for many of us, we get lost and forget who we are. "Astral gravity" makes it easy to pick up negative thoughts and beliefs about ourselves and others because they're literally all around us. Collectively they are the norm, and, unfortunately, this consciousness is so familiar that we just keep repeating the same cycles. We get spun around and around, caught up in all of the Maya/illusion of living in this world of polarity. Our true nature escapes us and, before we know it, we have bought into the negative conditioning that has been handed down generationally through our society, culture, and family.

Embodying and embracing our true divine nature is possible for us, but we need some help to get there. Love, wisdom, and strength are the three energies necessary for us at this time of Kaliyuga, and this is what Divine Mother Narayani embodies. She is the Trimurti (Triple Goddess) of Lakshmi (love, wealth, and abundance of all good things), Saraswati (wisdom, creativity, and the arts), and Durga or Kali (strength and protection).

Kali Durga is the powerful energy of divine strength and protection, and She helps us walk through the valley of fear. Kali Durga provides us with the inner strength to do the right thing even when it's hard. When we try to change self-defeating behaviors and the pull to go back to old behavior is strong, She helps us stand in the fire of transformation and shed the old skin. She is fierce and formidable to Her enemies and has no problem destroying the old to herald in new beginnings. She is exquisitely merciful and helps to lob the head off the egos of Her disciples. She is liberation personified and, with Her, one will blaze the trail to freedom. Kali Narayani is very comfortable in darkness as She is one with it All, which makes Her potent for clearing diseases and negative energy of any kind. Kali Durga will burn away all ignorance and delusion and strip you bare, leaving only your big, beautiful, blazing soul to illuminate the world.

OM Kali Durga!

Saraswati is that aspect of Divine Mother who is the teacher or guru of all gurus. She easily discerns truth from falsehood and, through Her wisdom, we can expand our consciousness and access higher levels of truth and understanding. She is the grace that fills the "pause" before we take action in any given moment. Saraswati helps us to see the multifaceted aspects of any situation and, through this clarity, helps to bestow compassion, wisdom, and understanding. She is the "respond rather than react" energy and blesses us all with creative expression, artistry, and the spoken word. Music is Her domain and She illuminates theatrics and artistic endeavors of all kinds. In a world where there is so much ignorance, Saraswati brings enlightened and inspired innovation to pierce even the thickest Maya. Collectively, we have been operating systems that are outdated and unhelpful to the planet and humanity. Saraswati will help to create the new paradigm and bring in a new earth.

OM Saraswati!

Lakshmi is the Goddess of all things good and wholesome. She is abundance personified and helps us to anchor beauty in our hearts and minds. Lakshmi's grace enables us to live rich and purposeful lives where we honor all aspects of our human birth and what it means to be embodied. To be blessed by Lakshmi means good health and wellbeing, spiritually, mentally, physically, and emotionally. Lakshmi ensures that everything you need will come to you at exactly the right time. She will activate the law of flow in life, and She is the result of one's churning the light and the dark within. She is the epitome of all things beautiful.

OM Lakshmi!

So the divine, in the form of the Triple Goddess Narayani, is the medicine we need for the new paradigm. To give you an understanding of Her vastness, the sun is only one of a million billion of Her creations. She is all-encompassing, loving, grace-filled, and merciful and is always there waiting for us to reach out and connect. Truth be told, She lives within us in the form of Sakthi, divine energy. One of the ways we access Her is through the principle of surrender. We cannot take any shortcuts on the spiritual path; there just really isn't such a thing. When we truly surrender, we will know Her. When we have the courage to feel our frozen emotions and heal our hearts, She becomes more awakened.

One of the ways we can do this is through working with the Inner Child Paradigm. When I started doing this work, I didn't understand the depth of the work and, I'm happy to say, it has deepened and expanded over the years. When I started checking in with my little girl in the early days, I would do it when I woke up in the morning, asking her things like, "How are you feeling?" "What do you need from me today?" This was the start of a reconnection with a part of myself that had been frozen in trauma and shame for a very long time. To be honest with you, I didn't get it back then, but I thought I'd do it anyway because people I respected and trusted were guiding me through the work. I'm so grateful I did because it has been the single most impactful healing modality I have in my spiritual toolkit.

So, my question to you is, do you have the courage to face the pain of yesterday? To allow all of your vulnerabilities to come up out of the darkness and into the light and touch the center of your pain and trauma? Are you willing to let yourself be naked before Her and let Her see every last piece of you? Where there is nothing to hide, nothing to keep, nothing to hold on to. Are you willing to surrender your preferences and your ideas in exchange for being given your heart's longing, a longing you didn't even know you had? To be flooded with your soul's purpose and divine calling in the world and to be fueled in that purpose by Her grace and Her Sakthi?

If you are reading these words, beloved, then She has heard your call and is bringing you close. I hope you stand in the fire of Her love and surrender everything you think you are and everything you think you have—give it all, hold nothing back. And may you rise like the phoenix gathering all you've been through as your sacred scriptures, may you listen to Her voice over all the other voices, may She call you home, and may She set your soul free.

Please join me in a sacred journey of the heart as we travel together to reclaim your inner child, call back your power, our preciousness, and your peace, and connect with Divine Mother Narayani, who dwells deep within you.

Om Namo Narayani
Jai Ma
With infinite love and blessings

Brahmankyrie xx

Activation

Close your eyes and come into your heart, take your awareness into the center of your chest to your heart chakra, Be aware of your breath. Take some deep breaths here and for a moment, acknowledge the profound miracle that is you.

Now take your awareness to the highest point in the universe, to the heart and mind of the divine, however you perceive the divine. Draw in the divine light from way above your head.

Pull this divine consciousness down through your body. Let yourself be illuminated in divine light. Then, take it all the way down and release it out of your feet and the base of your spine.

Now draw the energy up again, from the earth mother, feel Her response. Pull the energy up through your feet and the base of the spine, and as you draw this energy up, feel your energy, waking up from the base of the spine, and feel it start to mingle with the feminine energy rising through your being. On the out-breath, release the energy out of the top of the crown chakra on the top of the head. Now draw in from above and below simultaneously and coalesce the energy into your heart chakra, let the consciousness and energy marry in the heart and exhale.

Invocation—I call on the supreme being Divine Father and Divine Mother God/Goddess. I call on the energy of Sri Sakthi Amma Narayani, OM Namo Narayani. I call on the love, light, and power that is inherent in the whole of creation. I call on my soul and my divine self, and today I ask for the highest and most loving healing to reconnect me with my inner child and the Divine Mother within. Through the grace of the Mother, so be it.

Now imagine you can walk into the center of your heart chakra. Imagine walking on a beautiful, cobbled path where the stones are cool beneath your feet, and the sun is warm on your face. You feel safe, and you feel secure. As you continue to walk on this cobblestone path, you reach a door. As you approach the door, it opens, and you find yourself in this beautiful landscape of lush green grass, beautiful trees, and all of your favourite flowers. This energy is pristine in this place, and you feel the love of the Mother all around you.

You continue to walk down this grassy knoll until you come to a little stream, and there is a footbridge that will take you from one side of the stream to the other. So you begin to walk across the footbridge and continue to make your way through the grassy field. Then up in the distance, you see a big oak tree and underneath the oak tree is a little bench and sitting on that bench is a little child. This is your inner child, beloved, this is the little boy or girl that has been in your heart your whole life, and they are yearning to connect with you now.

In your mind's eye, make your way over to them and sit down next to them on the bench. Let them know how sorry you are that it has taken you so long to come back and get them. Spend some time being with them and let them know that you will not leave them.

Place your hand on your heart chakra and tune in to how you are feeling in your body. Say quietly to yourself. "I now release all negative thoughts, feelings, vibrations, and emotions from my mind, body, and energy field." Breathe in and release all over.

Now allow your inner child to guide you back through time and space to an experience they might be holding on to that they feel they need to release. Feel yourself surrounded by divine energy and protection. Allow those old feelings to come up in your mind-body and energy field and say, "I now release all pain and trauma from this experience and all experiences like it. I release the belief that I am not safe, and I chose to feel, heal, and surrender this energy now, through the grace of Mother Narayani, so be it." Breathe in and release all over. Allow the energy to leave the cells of your body. You may feel rushes of energy, emotion, or tingling;

sometimes, the clearing happens later on. Whatever your experience, just know that the divine is helping to transmute this stuck emotion and liberate you and your inner child into a new vibrational kingdom.

Once you have done this, in your mind's eye, in the particular memory, find your inner child. Normally when there has been pain and trauma, there is a split that happens between the emotional body and the mind. Part of liberating the inner child and reclaiming them is to find them in the memory and draw them close to your heart.

When you have found them in the memory, call them into your heart and say, "Beloved little one, you are the most important person in my life. I love you, I see you, I hear you, and now that I've found you, I'm never leaving you. You are safe, and I am going to love and protect you, through the grace of Mother Narayani, so be it." Place your hand on your heart chakra and breathe in. Send them all the love and nurturing they never received in that moment and reassure them they are safe.

Spend some time here being present to how you feel, being available to your inner child, and the process of reconnection. Allow the positive vibrations to ripple out through your mind, body, and energy field and allow this energy to fill up your space and permeate the area where you live. Remind your inner child that they are back in the present moment and all is well.

Repeat the mantra, "I love, trust, respect, accept, and honor myself exactly as I am. I am a divine child of God, and I am worthy of a beautiful life filled with love, joy, happiness, peace, and prosperity. Through the grace of Mother Narayani, so be it!"

Again, feel the positive vibrations permeate your consciousness and all around you. Thank Divine Mother Narayani for supporting deep healing and expansion, and when you're ready, you can open your eyes.

Om Namo Narayani

Jai Ma!

Journal and Integrate

1. What have you been triggered around lately? This will give you a good idea of where your inner child might be stuck and where to look in your consciousness to liberate them.

2. *Daily check-ins with your inner child will help you embody more emotional mastery and inner peace. How is your inner child feeling today? What do they need from you?*

- Divine Feminine Aligned Journal -

Free Gift

DIVINE MOTHER NARAYANI GROUP HEALING ACTIVATION

In this session we explore how to hold our energy; we clear pain and trauma from our past and liberate our inner child to expand into more light, love, and power.

Access here >> eventbrite.com/e/divine-mother-narayani-group-healing-tickets-152167492065

Om Namo Narayani

Biography

BRAHMANKYRIE is a spiritual teacher and healer in Encinitas, CA and spends most of her time running the Narayani Temple California and serving the incarcerated population at Donovan State Prison. Her life wasn't always a spiritual one, and after getting clean and sober in August 2006, she has spent the last 16 years sharing her story, teaching meditation and mantra, and healing people worldwide. Brahmankyrie is devoted to her path and lives her life in service to the divine.

Learn more at www.thebrahmanproject.com.

The Love Warrior

by Lettie Sullivan

Goddess energy is rising on the planet right now as many beings are answering the call within them to pick up the sword for justice and peace in our society.

Change begins with one single act of bravery- surrender and pushing into the rebirth.

Activating the release of the toxic status quo and the willingness to embrace change is a step we must deliberately initiate to reach the societal shift into collective trauma healing that is long overdue.

Stand back and witness your behavior patterns objectively. Notice your thoughts, feelings, and emotions. Nothing can be changed until it is identified and named. You have all the information to move forward, one step at a time.

The Sacred Feminine/Goddess energy is an embodied emotional, mental, and spiritual state.

To dance with this state of Being is to be in a sensorial concert that is harmonious—all of your senses activated.

But we're conditioned to be more comfortable in our thinking minds because being in our bodies can be super uncomfortable.

Being with whatever is showing up during conversations around systemic oppression without jumping to a conclusion, numbing out with distractions, or outright denial is essential—that's where the real work is.

Our ancestors left us with unfinished business. We can remedy traumas of the past by healing ourselves first, and then sharing our healing vibrations with others.

When confronted about matters of caste privilege, race, gender norms, or "Other-ism" do you know how to respond?

What if you could stand confidently in these conversations with fierce compassion and resolve?

How do you want to BE going forward, in relation to dismantling systems of oppression and being a crucial element in the building of a society centered on justice and equality?

Let's activate the Love Warrior in our consciousness so that we can pioneer social interactions that celebrate our differences—without taking a bypass of the history, the hurt, and the shame.

It requires the capacity to stand in the gap between deep forgiveness and fierce accountability.

Like Fannie Lou Hamer said, "Nobody's free until everybody's free."

"Nobody's free until everybody's free."

~Lou Hamer

Activation

THE LOVE WARRIOR ARCHETYPE DEFINED

Love warriors have heart.

H. E. A. R. T.

The H stands for the healing presence that love warriors emanate: a vibrational frequency of healing, health, and wholeness.

The E stands for empathy: being open and receptive. The deep empathy for yourself and humanity.

The A stands for acceptance: acceptance in an objective sense, as in being tuned in and discerning what's real with a capital R.

The R stands for resolute: resolute in your regard for yourself, for life, for humanity, and for the earth, resolute in your vision, resolute in your faith. A reverential revolutionary.

The T stands for transmute and transform. Being very intentional about how you show up and what you do with the energy that surrounds you.

Love warriors have heart. They are a beneficial presence on the planet.

The embodiment of love, power, and grace. Willing to speak truth to power with compassion and clarity.

Love Warriors are clear in their values and have a strong moral compass, exhibit critical thinking, groundedness, and equanimity.

Journal and Integrate

Recall a situation where you had to stand up for yourself and/or another. What do you remember about the sensations in your body?

How did you process the situation after the fact? Were you satisfied/ dissatisfied with your response?

If you had to do it over again, what would you do differently?

Free Gift

THE FOUR AGREEMENTS OF DIVERSE SPACES

This workshop is designed to be a catalyst to a deeper inquiry about what signals you are emitting into the space you're holding. One of the most important actions you can take in service to holding a room with people from many different backgrounds, cultures, and gender presentation is to ground first yourself, then the space and everyone in it.

Access here >> **bit.ly/DC_4Aworkshop**

Biography

LETTIE SULLIVAN is a Priestess of the Sacred Arts and the Creatrix of the Goddess Ministry, whose mission is to anchor energetic activism centered in Love, Divine Feminine wisdom, metaphysical principles, and cosmic time cycles. Lettie is also an inspirational speaker, a professional organizer, a life coach, and an author.

Learn more at **lettiesullivan.com.**

The Temple Body Priestess

by Sofiah Thom

The Temple Body Priestess represents the embodiment of living in devotion to divine purpose. She offers her Temple Body as a vessel of love and recognizes herself as an instrument of the divine. She lives by her word with absolute integrity. You may hear her whispering to you from deep within to embody your sovereign power. This whisper is the power that she holds in her womb and her blood. She's able to rewrite any story that holds her to the past. She knows that she is here to leave a legacy and awaken humanity with her presence, voice, and dance. She knows that her body is a Temple and that her life is a living prayer of gratitude. She creates from a place of empowered pleasure.

She is a modern-day Temple Dancer, Alchemist, and Songstress. She is a powerful mirror, holding space, amplifying, initiating, and awakening humanity with her body, voice, and dance. Like an alchemist, she holds power to transmute old stories into gold. As a songstress channeling her intentions through her sound, she creates a resonant field of healing.

The Temple Body Priestess teaches each of us to recognize our multidimensional beingness and our capacity to use our sexual creative energy to create the life that we vision for ourselves. She recognizes her sovereign power and knows that she has dominion over her body, her sexuality, her space, her domain, and everything that she's creating. She harnesses the power of her Sword of Discernment and cuts away what misaligns with who she truly is. With her focused presence and attention, she creates the boundaries and structures that support her in fully living out her divine purpose and serving the awakening of humanity.

It takes time to own and embody the Temple Body Priestess, who knows how to harness her feminine power and magnetize all she desires. The energy lies dormant within and will come through when you are ready and when the world is ready. The Temple Body Priestess shows herself through the wisdom of experience held in your body, which happens over time. Her power has nothing to do with her outer appearance but with inner experience and a cultivated relationship with her body, sexuality, spirituality, and creativity. She is humble and does not fit any standard or stereotype. She is comfortable in her skin, releases any comparison, and celebrates collaboration. She treats her body as a sanctuary, an altar to worship, remember, and feel pleasure. Awake in her senses, she may be dressed in fabrics soft and sensual to the touch, anointed with scented oils, or adorning her Temple Body in her unique way.

Like all archetypes, the Temple Body Priestess looks and feels different for each of us.

The Temple Body Priestess revealed herself to me over time through challenges, initiations, and awakenings throughout my life. I first recognized her power within me on a vision quest to discover my signature soul essence. Through this journey, I discovered the infinite creative power held within my womb. Years later, I moved through an initiation of a miscarriage that almost took my life. This miscarriage brought me even deeper into my womb wisdom. I had for many years questioned my purpose and the work I was here to offer to the world. The miscarriage awakened me to my purpose as a spiritual midwife. It spurred me to claim my path as a Temple Body Priestess to initiate women as Embodied Feminine Leaders, called to birth a new paradigm collectively.

Throughout my life, I have practiced and cultivated many different healing arts and modalities. These practices have given me outlets to express the Temple Body Priestess within me. All along, she was whispering to me and guiding me where to bring my precious energy and attention. By listening to her, I uncovered the unique gifts I needed to cultivate the expression of my full potential. Through deep self-exploration, the Temple Body Priestess revealed herself to me as my Signature Essence.

We are in the midst of a revolution. The old paradigms and old constructs are breaking down. There is something new birthing, and we must find a new way of creating our lives as women, especially as Soulpreneurs and visionaries.

We each have masculine and feminine energies within us. As Embodied Feminine Leaders, we are birthing a new paradigm. We have to have both principles awakened within us and be in the right relationship with masculine and feminine energies. The masculine and feminine cannot live without the other. Together they are the sacred marriage, the dance of shiva and shakti. To give birth to a new paradigm, calling both the feminine and masculine energies within us into balance, is an absolute necessity.

We have to be willing to ask ourselves, "Am I showing up fully aligned with my essence in a way that honors me and my body? Am I prioritizing self-care and filling my cup first?" So that when we're speaking, when we're inspiring, when we're creating movements in the world, we are living with total integrity with what we teach. We have to be diligent, checking in with ourselves constantly. As we step out and come into our full power as feminine leaders, there is so much that we have to do to create a wave, and so we also have to know how to honor our rhythm as women, with the moon, and within our wombs. We need to rewrite these stories passed down for generations around what it means to be a woman that puts everyone else before herself. We have to learn to put ourselves first and recognize that we have to fill our own cups first, especially as a feminine leader birthing a new paradigm.

Much of our world sees through the patriarchal lens of having a goal and a plan, focusing on what there is to gain and "what's in it for me," but it's time to do things differently. We are not necessarily going to know what that looks like. This journey is about trusting and being guided from within and connecting to the divine creative spirit to guide us. The Temple Body Priestess supports us to be in absolute devotion to being guided by the divine.

If we tune in, the wisdom of our body guides us in every present moment. Our body and our voice are our instruments of the divine, and we have to keep our instruments tuned. Through our bodies, we express ourselves and create our lives. By taking care of our body, we keep it rightfully tuned. When something is out of alignment, our body will communicate with us and let us know when we need to slow down and listen. Our body is our teacher, and the wisdom within us is here to guide us. We must take the time to listen.

Each one of us has our path and divine purpose. When we get out of our own way, we will see that what we do is not about ourselves but about being in service to something greater. We must choose to live in devotion to our service, even when we're not sure what that is yet. By devoting each day to listening and being guided by what turns you on and what lights you up, you will become more and more aware of the subtle clues that have been guiding you all along the way.

Choose to show up in service and devotion to the divine creative spirit that wants to flow through you naturally. When you open up to receive, that's when all the magic flows. It's beyond what we can see or think. The Temple Body Priestess shows us that beautiful magic unfolds when we offer ourselves to a life of devotion.

Activation

A Sword of Discernment Practice to Connect with your Inner Temple Body Priestess

Carve out twenty minutes for this practice.

Prepare your Temple Body to receive. Every moment is an opportunity to create a ritual. As you prepare for this practice, cleanse yourself with sage or palo santo, clear your thoughts, and come into the frequency of your highest desires. Adorn yourself in a way that makes you feel like the divine feminine being that you are. Dress in a way that pleases you. Anoint yourself with delicious scents, and treat your body like the altar that it is.

To begin this practice, I invite you to play the song, Sword of Discernment, by Myself and Heather Christie, on Spotify. You can access the song here: spoti.fi/3gtytG5.

Close your eyes, if that feels comfortable for you, and connect in with the rise and fall of your breath.

Bring your awareness into your womb, imagining a beautiful lotus flower in your pelvis. I like to call it the lotus flower Yoni portal. She is the portal into your temple body. See your lotus flower rooted deep into the earth, deeply connected to the core of Mama Gaia.

And then bring your awareness into your crown chakra at the top of the skull. Open up your crown for the divine creative spirit to flow down through you, feeling the channel from your sacred lotus roots and all the way up to your crown.

Next, connect with your inner cross, where the horizontal and vertical aspects of the masculine and feminine energies meet at the center of your chest. Visualize a brilliant diamond or gem at the center of your heart, where the sacred marriage unites. This gem holds the space of your divine essence. See the inner diamond or gem of your divine essence shining brilliantly.

Now connect to your inner Temple Body Priestess. What messages does she have for you? How does she desire to express herself through you?

Invite any movement that wants to come, perhaps spiraling the hips, allowing the body to move and express itself as the

Temple Body Priestess. Connect with your wholeness and your inherent innocence, and know that you have everything you need within your Temple Body to create the life you envision. Feel this vision that the Temple Body Priestess is calling forth within you and where she calls you to devote yourself and your presence at this time.

As you listen to her messages, I invite you to begin humming, opening to receive the frequency of the Temple Body Priestess. Allow her to express through your sounds or tones, in whatever way she decides to reveal herself, with any message she may have for you at this time.

See and feel yourself as the Temple Body Priestess embodied, and then visualize yourself with your Sword of Discernment. With your sword, you have the power to cut away what no longer serves and to create the boundaries and structures that support who you are becoming and who you were born to be. Come into presence, attention, and focus so that everything you do aligns with what you desire to create and who you desire to become on this path of evolution.

Connecting with your heart, feel yourself as divine love embodied. Breathe and notice how you feel in your body. In closing, offer gratitude to the Temple Body Priestess within you. Thank her for all the wisdom she shared with you. When you are ready, gently come back into the present moment.

Journal and Integrate

What did you discover in your experience with the Sword of Discernment Practice to Connect with your Inner Temple Body Priestess? Write, stream of consciousness for five minutes.

What aspects of the Temple Body Priestess are you ready to activate within you?

Reflect on your relationship with the divine masculine and feminine energies within you. How would you like to improve your relationship with both the masculine and the feminine?

What do you need to cut away with your Sword of Discernment to live in alignment with who you desire to be?

— Divine Feminine Aligned Journal —

Free Gift

DIVINE PURPOSE

Enjoy this 20-minute guided dance journey to awaken your Temple Body to your Divine Purpose. Allow yourself to play and explore. Feel into all that you desire, and let yourself take up space as you allow your divine essence to flow in your unique way. Move and express in a way that embodies your Divine purpose.

Access here >> sofiahthom.pages.ontraport.net/divinepurposegiftoptin

Biography

SOFIAH THOM is a divine feminine mentor and leader for leaders birthing a new paradigm. An author, modern-day temple dancer, and entrepreneur committed to guiding women to embody their feminine power and birth their gifts into the world.

Creator and CEO of the Temple Body Arts™ School for Embodied Feminine Leadership, Sofiah mentors women to create a life aligned with their essence and create the impact and income they desire while supporting the Rise of the Divine.

Sofiah is co-author of The Path of the Priestess Book: Discover Your Divine Purpose. She has been teaching, speaking, and performing in-person and online around the globe for over 20 years. Driven by her lifelong passion for dance, creative expression, and feminine spirituality, Sofiah creates a safe and powerful container for recognizing one's creative potential and power through sacred movement and inner exploration.

Alongside her husband Brendan and a handful of visionaries, Sofiah co-founded the Envision Festival in Costa Rica, a conscious festival celebrating music, art, and sacred movement.

Together, Sofiah and her husband co-founded Danyasa Eco-Retreat in the beautiful beach town of Dominical, Costa Rica, where they live.

Learn more at **sofiahthom.com**.

Lakshmi

by Patrina Wisdom

My relationship with Goddess Lakshmi's energy is everything! I am an embodiment of Lakshmi. She is the goddess of wealth, fortune, love, beauty, joy, and prosperity. The eternal mother. I would not have been able to recreate my life in such a powerful way after losing my husband to suicide if the spirit of Lakshmi had not shown me the way.

It is so important for us as women to harness the power of our innate femininity. Own the truth of who we BE and create an abundant life from that space. Physical wealth, accomplishments, or accolades do not define us. However, standing in our power and purpose, coming out of hiding, and showing up to do God's work does.

It's our birthright to be prosperous and abundant. We cannot serve from an empty cup or empty pockets. Open yourself to receive more so you can give more and experience the fullness of life that Spirit intended for you.

Activation

One of the most important things you can do to improve your financial situation is to understand your money story.

"Money is GOD in action."

It's important to analyze your existing relationship with money—what you are saying about money, how you feel about it, what you believe about it, and how you use it.

We often believe that it's external factors that are hindering us from creating wealth. Truth is... Your thoughts and beliefs about money have created your current financial reality.

The following activation will help bring awareness to the root cause of your blockages to abundance (relational, financial, etc.) and will reconnect you to your earliest experience of freedom, fulfillment, and peace.

I invite you to find a quiet space in your home, office, or out in nature. Once you've found that sacred space I want you to sit in a comfortable position and take 3 slow and deep cleansing breaths. Breathe in love... and breathe out any tension, stress, or anxiety that you may be holding in your body.

Get grounded and allow yourself to be completely present. Release the activities of the day and any emotions, feelings or memories within yourself that you may be holding onto consciously or unconsciously.

Now close your eyes and allow yourself to go back to a simpler time when you were young and had no expectations or responsibilities.

Visualize yourself at your freest age. Maybe you were three or four, maybe you were twenty five, or twenty eight years old. Just tap into the time when you felt the most free.

What were the conditions? What was your thought process?

What was the self talk that you were experiencing? What was going on in your life that enabled you to feel so free?

Be with that feeling of freedom. Take a series of deep breaths here and feel into this embodiment of freedom.

When you're ready, move to a time when you felt the most powerful.

What were the conditions? What were the thoughts you had?

What conversations did you have with yourself and others?

What was the mindset or circumstances that helped you to feel so powerful? What were the beliefs, identity, or support that helped you to feel and embody your personal power?

How did it feel to be in your full power? What is possible if you brought that energy of personal power into your life now?

Take a couple of deep breaths here, breathe power in, hold it for a few counts and then lock that feeling in.

Next I want you to think of a time when you felt the most safe, protected, nurtured, loved and taken care of? A time when you were full of hope, faith, and inspiration.

What was going on? Was this feeling of safety intrinsic or was it from something or someone outside of yourself?

Journal and Integrate

1. On a scale of 1-10 (10 being GREAT), rate your relationship with yourself. _____
2. On a scale of 1-10 (10 being GREAT), rate your relationship with money. _____
3. Did you talk about money in your home? What memories do you have of your parents discussing money?

4. Did your family experience a defining moment around money? A defining moment shapes our beliefs—we take away from that experience a meaning. What did you make that experience mean?

Free Gift

ABUNDANCE BREAKTHROUGH & FINANCIAL ASSESSMENT

A 60 minute LIVE Call on Zoom Videoconference to Identify and Breakthrough your blocks to Abundance. In our time together, we will discuss your financial goals and dreams, and blocks that are keeping you from creating abundance in your life.

We will assess where you are currently in relation to your desires. If appropriate, I will then gather information about your expenses, debt, life/health insurance, retirement, etc. in order to make appropriate recommendations for moving forward.

Access here >> bit.ly/AbundanceAssessment

Biography

PATRINA WISDOM is an Amazon Best-selling author, speaker, Wealth Mentor, and creator of the Badass Bodacious Life Movement. She believes that in order to live a BadAss Bodacious Life, you must connect with, embrace, and exercise every part of yourself.

After losing her husband of 20 years to suicide in 2009 and learning that she was pregnant with her fourth child the same day, Patrina Wisdom took her personal story and decades of experience as an entrepreneur and business leader and began the process of creating her Badass Bodacious Life.

Learn more at **Patrinawisdom.com.**

More books by Flower of Life Press

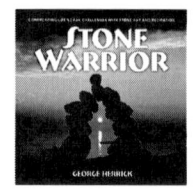

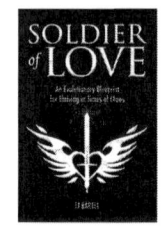

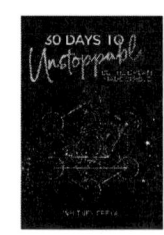

www.floweroflifepress.com

Made in United States
North Haven, CT
08 August 2022